1

Ple

Dunkirk and the Fall of France

Campaign Chronicles

Dunkirk and the Fall of France

Geoffrey Stewart

Campaign Chronicle
Series Editor

Christopher Summerville

Pen & Sword
MILITARY

First published in Great Britain in 2008 by
Pen & Sword Military
An imprint of
Pen & Sword Books Ltd
47 Church Street
Barnsley
South Yorkshire
S70 2AS

Copyright © Geoffrey Stewart

ISBN 978 1 84415 803 4

A CIP catalogue record for this book is available from the British Library.

Typeset in 11pt Sabon by Mac Style, Beverley, East Yorkshire
Printed and bound in the UK by CPI

Pen & Sword Books Ltd incorporates the imprints of Pen & Sword Aviation, Pen & Sword Maritime, Pen & Sword Military, Wharncliffe Local History, Pen & Sword Select, Pen & Sword Military Classics, Leo Cooper, Remember When, Seaforth Publishing and Frontline Publishing

For a complete list of Pen & Sword titles please contact
PEN & SWORD BOOKS LIMITED
47 Church Street, Barnsley, South Yorkshire, S70 2AS, England
E-mail: enquiries@pen-and-sword.co.uk
Website: www.pen-and-sword.co.uk

Contents

Contents

List of Maps

List of Illustrations

———◆———

Dunkirk and the Fall of France

Preface

This account does not rest on new and original research but it does reflect a growing perception that the dramatic events of spring 1940 can be looked at afresh. The popular portrait of a decadent France going down shamefully to a superior Nazi Germany has become an enduring legend, most recently finding expression in the phrase, in use in the United States during the Iraq War, that the French were 'cheese-eating, surrender monkeys'. By contrast, the same traditional mythology sanctified Dunkirk as a British triumph, laying the seeds of ultimate victory over the Nazi monster. The roots of both views lie in the wartime needs of a Britain standing alone in June 1940. Churchill's famous account of his meeting in Paris on 16 May firmly places the blame on French military incompetence. In the decades after 1945 explanations were sought in either the decadence of French inter-war society, the bitter political divisions of left and right or, most charitably, in the bloodletting of 1914–1918.

Whatever explanation was emphasised, there seemed to be a consensus that France was doomed. Such a view was most graphically offered in the outstanding television series, *World at War*. The mellifluous yet potent voice of the narrator, Sir Laurence Olivier, gave a new generation of students and viewers the received wisdom in Episode 3, a superior Germany inevitably triumphing over a doomed France.

Part of the problem lies in the proper tendency of historians to look for explanations and seek causes, the more deep-seated the better. The role of chance and human foibles tends to be downplayed. Yet in war, contingent factors are often the decisive ones. Many recent studies of the 1940 campaign have stressed the high risks involved in the German attack. Adam Tooze, in his recent magisterial study of the German war economy, points out:

> a close analysis of the mechanics of the Blitzkrieg reveals the astonishing degree of concentration achieved, but also the

enormous gamble that Hitler and the Wehrmacht leadership were taking on 10 May. Precisely because it involved such a concentrated use of force, Manstein's plan was a 'one shot affair'. If the initial assault had failed, and it could have failed in many ways, the Wehrmacht as an offensive force would have been spent.

Had this occurred, historians would have spent years in analysis of the fundamental weaknesses of the Third Reich and the brittle nature of morale in certain key Wehrmacht units, instead of doing this to the Third Republic and its army. Many French units fought heroically at various times in the campaign. Some German units displayed panic and pessimism. This was easy to understand, as shells from German tanks bounced harmlessly off the heavily armoured French Char B tanks. The war was lost by the French largely as a result of a series of touch-and-go encounters, when the actions of individuals – and sheer luck – influenced the outcome. Certainly mistakes by the French High Command played a part but then the German High Command and Hitler made mistakes at various points. Likewise, the British got away at Dunkirk as a result of a combination of factors, involving luck with the weather, German errors, and dogged French fighting in and around Lille.

When the campaign began on 10 May it is worth remembering that French defeat was not inevitable. Very few on the German side believed a crushing victory was possible, let alone likely. It has been said that only Guderian, Manstein and Hitler were optimistic, but even Hitler at times showed attacks of nerves, indicating that his optimism was fragile. As so often before and later, he was 'going for broke'. This time the gamble paid off. It need not have done.

York 2007

Maps

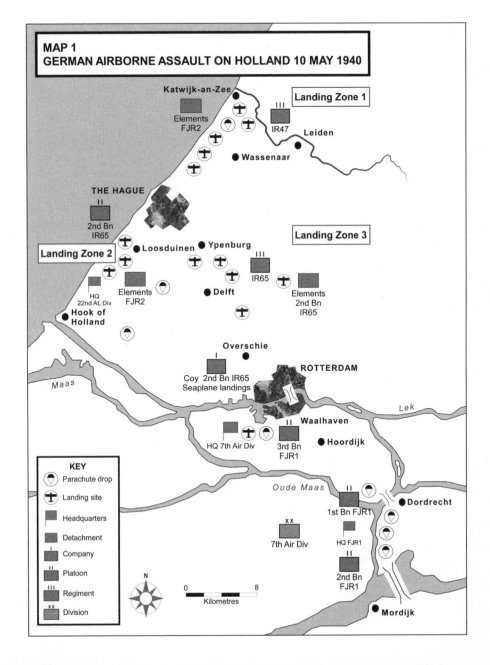

MAP 1
GERMAN AIRBORNE ASSAULT ON HOLLAND 10 MAY 1940

Katwijk-an-Zee

Elements FJR2

Landing Zone 1

IR47

Leiden

Wassenaar

THE HAGUE

2nd Bn IR65

Landing Zone 2

Landing Zone 3

Loosduinen

Ypenburg

IR65

HQ 22nd AL Div

Elements FJR2

Delft

Elements 2nd Bn IR65

Hook of Holland

Overschie

ROTTERDAM

Coy 2nd Bn IR65 Seaplane landings

Maas

Lek

Waalhaven

HQ 7th Air Div

3rd Bn FJR1

Hoordijk

Oude Maas

Dordrecht

1st Bn FJR1

7th Air Div

HQ FJR1

2nd Bn FJR1

Mordijk

KEY
- Parachute drop
- Landing site
- Headquarters
- Detachment
- I Company
- II Platoon
- III Regiment
- XX Division

N

0   8
Kilometres

Dunkirk and the Fall of France

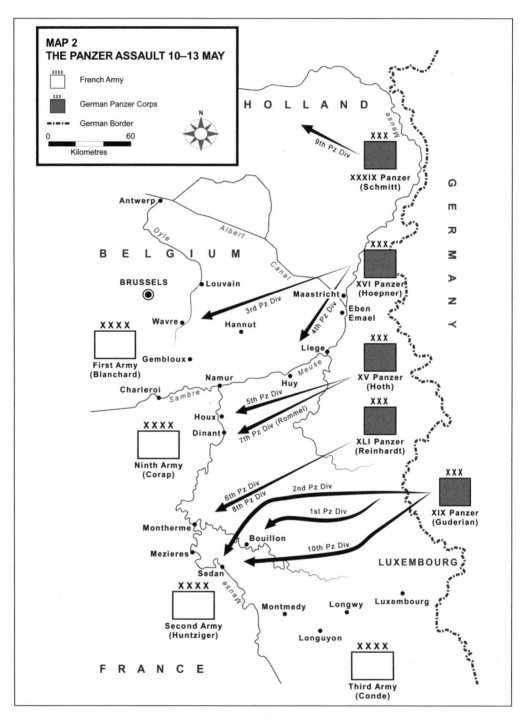

MAP 2
THE PANZER ASSAULT 10–13 MAY

French Army

German Panzer Corps

German Border

0   60
Kilometres

N

HOLLAND

GERMANY

9th Pz Div

XXX
XXXIX Panzer
(Schmitt)

Antwerp

Dyle

Albert

Canal

BELGIUM

BRUSSELS

Louvain

Maastricht

XXX
XVI Panzer
(Hoepner)

Eben
Emael

3rd Pz Div

Wavre

Hannut

4th Pz Div

Liege

XXX
XV Panzer
(Hoth)

XXXX
First Army
(Blanchard)

Gembloux

Namur

Huy

Meuse

Charleroi

Sambre

5th Pz Div

Houx

7th Pz Div (Rommel)

Dinant

XXX
XLI Panzer
(Reinhardt)

XXXX
Ninth Army
(Corap)

6th Pz Div

8th Pz Div

2nd Pz Div

1st Pz Div

XXX
XIX Panzer
(Guderian)

Montherme

Bouillon

10th Pz Div

Mezieres

LUXEMBOURG

Sedan

Meuse

XXXX
Second Army
(Huntziger)

Montmedy

Longwy

Luxembourg

Longuyon

XXXX
Third Army
(Conde)

FRANCE

xvi

Maps

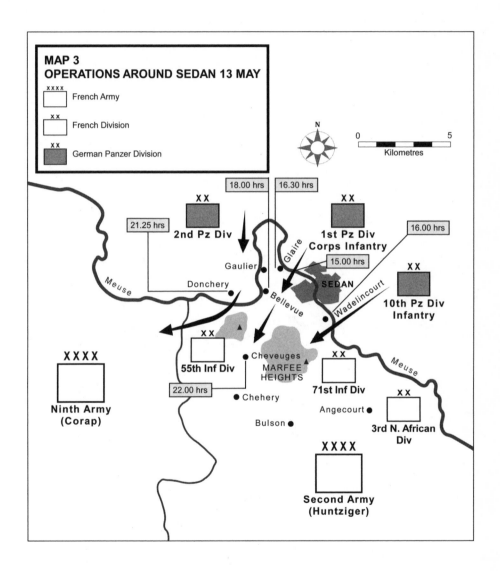

MAP 3
OPERATIONS AROUND SEDAN 13 MAY

French Army

French Division

German Panzer Division

2nd Pz Div

1st Pz Div
Corps Infantry

10th Pz Div
Infantry

55th Inf Div

71st Inf Div

3rd N. African
Div

Ninth Army
(Corap)

Second Army
(Huntziger)

18.00 hrs

16.30 hrs

21.25 hrs

16.00 hrs

15.00 hrs

22.00 hrs

Gaulier

Doncherry

Bellevue

SEDAN

Glaire

Wadelincourt

Meuse

Meuse

Cheveuges

MARFEE
HEIGHTS

Chehery

Bulson

Angecourt

N

0   5
Kilometres

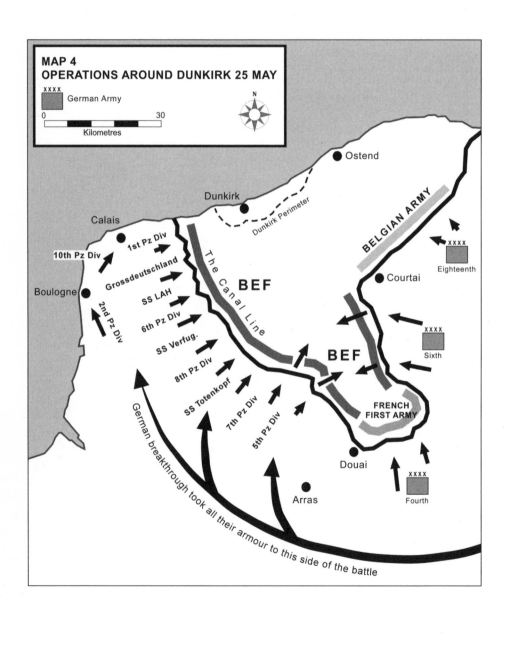

MAP 4
OPERATIONS AROUND DUNKIRK 25 MAY

Maps

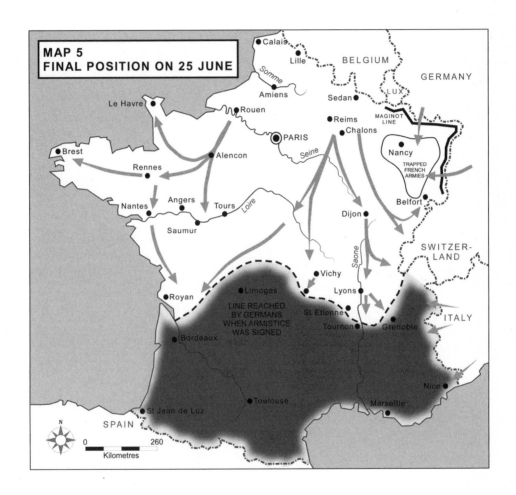

MAP 5
FINAL POSITION ON 25 JUNE

Calais
Lille
BELGIUM
GERMANY
Somme
Amiens
Sedan
LUX
Le Havre
Rouen
Reims
MAGINOT
LINE
PARIS
Chalons
Nancy
Brest
Alencon
Seine
TRAPPED
FRENCH
ARMIES
Rennes
Belfort
Nantes
Angers
Tours
Loire
Dijon
Saumur
SWITZER-
LAND
Saone
Vichy
Royan
Limoges
Lyons
LINE REACHED
BY GERMANS
WHEN ARMISTICE
WAS SIGNED
St Etienne
ITALY
Tournon
Grenoble
Bordeaux
Nice
St Jean de Luz
Toulouse
Marseille
N
SPAIN
0   260
Kilometres

Background

The Legacy of 1914–1918

In 1914 seven massive German armies had assaulted France. The most powerful – the ones that were to provide the hammer blow of victory – swung in a wide arc through Belgium, aiming to envelop the five armies of France and crush the Republic in a six-week campaign. This famous plan of von Schlieffen failed – but only just. Mistakes were made and a gap opened between the First and Second German Armies, enabling a triumphant French counter-attack to the east of Paris – the 'miracle' of the Marne. The Germans retreated to the River Aisne and dug in. Attempts by both sides to outflank the other led to a line of trenches from the Swiss border to the Channel. A four-year war of attrition followed, bleeding all the participants of their young men as they sought to break the deadlock. Both sides experimented. The Germans tried gas. It added to the horrors of life in the trenches but was indecisive. The British invented the tank and used it to limited effect for the first time on the Somme in September 1916. However, the machines were too slow, 1–2 miles per hour, and too mechanically unreliable to achieve a real breakthrough. Carefully orchestrated creeping artillery barrages were developed and French, German, and British engineers rapidly pushed the evolution of air power. Perhaps the Battle of Cambrai in 1917 should be seen as seminal in explaining 1940. On the one hand the British seemed to achieve a notable victory by using tanks, but the Germans then recaptured most of the lost ground using their new 'stormtrooper' assault tactics. Put the two together and the Blitzkrieg of the 1940s emerged. The Germans in 1918 applied their approach and seemed to have found a method of breakthrough with a mixture of short sharp thunderstorms of artillery fire wedded to rapid infantry assaults by elite stormtroopers. The five great offensives of 1918 rocked the Allies but ultimately failed with vast loss of life for the German attackers, and between August and November they were driven back by a series of offensives spearheaded by the now formidable British Army.

There is a tendency to exaggerate the national differences in the responses to the experience of mass murder on the Western Front. The prevalent British tradition is to see the Western Front either through the eyes of the war poets or the famous television comedy *Blackadder Goes Forth* – views that may be summarised as 'mud, blood and incompetence'. Such a view has been heavily and effectively criticised recently by Gordon Corrigan in his aptly titled *Mud, Blood and Poppycock*. It is worth remembering that there were memoirists and writers who celebrated British success in the First World War and that, ultimately, Britain had won the war with the largest army the country ever produced and the largest air force and navy in the world. Likewise, with regard to France, there is a tendency to see the war as in some ways breaking the national spirit and in this way explaining defeat in 1940. The 1.4 million dead and the millions of 'mutilés' are facts presented as obscuring victory. In fact many Frenchmen felt justly proud of the victory and its reversal of the humiliation of 1870. France was once again the dominant power in Europe. By comparison there is a tendency to view the German response through the words and ideas of Hitler or, at least, Nationalist writers like Ernst Jünger. However, for every Hitler or Jünger there were writers and artists, mainly on the left of the political spectrum, who emphasised the horrors of war much like the British war poets. The most famous of these was, of course, Erich Maria Remarque, in his best-seller, *All Quiet on the Western Front*. German expressionist painters in the 1920s populated their canvases with cripples and deformities arising from the war. In other words, all three countries saw mixed responses to the horrors of 1914–1918 and what happened then did not determine events in the second great conflict but it certainly influenced them.

All the key German decision makers in 1940 had been conditioned by their experiences in the First World War and sought to learn from this experience. What was learned depended on where you were in 1914–1918 and which side you were on. Hitler knew the realities of trench warfare as well as any of these decision makers, having served continuously for the whole four years as a battalion messenger. He was also keenly aware of the cracking of the German home front

Background

under the impact of the strains induced by a long war. His enthusiasm for the Manstein plan in February 1940, in place of that offered by the senior army planners, arose from the promise it held of avoiding the stalemate of a war of attrition and delivering Germany a quick victory. It was risky but on balance suited Germany's needs and matched Hitler's desire to avoid a repetition of 1914.

Other Germans were also anxious to avoid a repetition of 1914, most importantly Heinz Guderian, a young signals officer in the First World War, and a soldier impressed by the potential of the tank. His early interest in radio communication was significant and his knowledge was a vital ingredient in the evolution of new doctrines of the command and control of tanks in battle. He was influenced by British writing on armoured warfare and when the Nazis came to power and began rapid rearmament, persuaded the regime to form three Panzer divisions in 1935. In 1937 he published *Achtung–Panzer!*, a hymn of praise to the potential of the tank, organised into swiftly moving mass units of surprise and destruction. His ideas were not fully accepted by the other senior generals but enjoyed some favour with Hitler and the Nazi politicians, who liked the image of speed, toughness and modernity. Other senior officers were more influenced by their wartime experiences of the technical limitations of the machines, which so often seemed to break down. In 1940, however, 'Hurrying Heinz', as he had become known, was to play a crucial part in achieving German victory in France as a Panzer corps commander. Commanding one of the Panzer divisions in 1940 was another famous German general who had learned his trade in the previous war, Erwin Rommel. Rommel had been a young stormtroop commander in 1918 and had made his name as an infantry expert. He was appointed to command the 7th Panzer Division in February 1940 with no real experience of armoured warfare: but he brought a belief in the explosive violence of the stormtrooper tactics of 1918, which fitted well with his new position and the potential of the tank.

The French, too, had learned lessons from 1914–1918. The French Army – not surprisingly in view of the French propensity for grand theory – had gone to war totally gripped by a doctrine which, in 1914, insisted on the offensive regardless of cost. It proved a disaster in the September of that year as the bodies of young French soldiers piled up before German defensive positions in eastern France. Out of this experience came a new theory that gripped the French High Command in 1939–1940. Now it was the doctrine of the methodical battle and the continuous front. The defensive was now uppermost and theory was literally given concrete form in the complex fortifications known as the Maginot Line, all along France's eastern border with Germany. There would be no headlong assault, simply the gradual build-up of pressure until the superior economic resources of Britain and France slowly crushed the German foe. The most important Frenchman in terms of military influence was General Maurice Gamelin, who, since his appointment as Chief of Staff in 1935, had supervised French rearmament, and in 1939 he became Commander-in-Chief. He was an experienced soldier who had served on Joffre's Staff in 1914 and was widely credited as the brains behind the successful French counter-offensive in that year. Highly intelligent, with an interest in art and philosophy, he was adept at handling difficult French politicians. In many ways he resembles such 'political' generals as Eisenhower and Marshall, whose reputations – unlike that of Gamelin – shone at the end of the Second World War. They, however, did not have to confront the Wehrmacht in 1940. In many ways, Gamelin's overall strategic approach was correct and far-sighted, for this was how the Allies finally beat the Third Reich. But in 1940 he made key mistakes, most notably misjudging the new German point of attack. He was right, in 1939, in judging it to be a replay of the Schlieffen Plan – which is exactly what the German General Staff came up with – and Gamelin planned sensible countermoves. Unfortunately for his reputation and the fate of France, Hitler changed the plan in February 1940. A cautious, methodical thinker, Gamelin could not conceive of his opponents taking the risk of an offensive through the Ardennes, and in this he was at one with most of the German General Staff.

The British had played a vital and increasing part in the defeat of Germany in 1914–1918 but the cost had been tremendous, with just under a million British and Commonwealth dead. This was less than the casualties suffered by the French and Germans, let alone the Russians, but for a country unused to such military commitment and slaughter it had a profound effect. 'Never again' became the catchphrase. Britain refused a formal alliance with

Background

France after the war and the British Army resumed its Victorian role as an imperial police force, scattered in penny packets across the globe. Britain, the leader in tank warfare, allowed its early advantages to slip away. Experiments in armoured warfare had continued through the 1920s and into the early 1930s. There was an appreciation of the importance of radio in command and control, and many of the lessons learned by the British Army were put into practice by Guderian in Germany. The financial squeeze on defence expenditure in the 1930s hit the army harder than the other two services and tank warfare was neglected. Britain refused to consider the idea of committing a major force to the continent. As the German threat grew, it was assumed that the French would do the fighting on land. Britain's Navy would blockade Germany and the expanding RAF threaten a bombing offensive. Only in February 1939 did the British Government finally agree to commit a 'Field Force' to France in the event of war. The result was an expeditionary force much inferior to that which had crossed the Channel in 1914. But then, most of the German High Command were convinced that the German Army of 1939 was much inferior in training and preparation to the one of 1914.

The other more minor participants in the events of 1940 were also influenced and conditioned by the events of the First World War. The Dutch had been left alone and remained neutral throughout the war. They hoped for a similar outcome in 1940. They were to be bitterly disappointed. Belgium had been invaded in 1914 and most of the country occupied other than a tiny corner in the west. Initially they drew the sensible conclusion that their best security lay in a close alliance with France and coordination of defence with their large neighbour to the south. The Franco-Belgian alliance remained in being until 1936, but following the German remilitarisation of the Rhineland in March of that year, the Belgian authorities declared their neutrality, thus candid and effective coordination with the French ceased. This was to add to the difficulties of an efficient riposte to a German assault in 1940.

The Coming of the Second World War
In 1919 Marshal Foch, the Supreme Allied Commander, had famously said of the Peace Treaty of that year, that it was armistice

for twenty years. Certainly the Second World War, in part, grew out of the widely held German view that the Treaty of Versailles was unfair and needed to be changed. In fact it had already been amended by the time Hitler came to power in 1933. The much-hated reparations that had been imposed on the vanquished Germany by the victors had been dropped the previous year and the small occupying forces in western Germany had been withdrawn five years early in 1930. There was every prospect of peacefully renegotiating the disarmament clauses that had reduced the old Imperial Army to 100,000 officers and men. Britain, in particular, felt that the Treaty of Versailles had been too harsh and had no appetite for enforcing it rigorously. With some grumbling, France was likely to acquiesce in any renegotiation that the British supported. In this sense it was not the Treaty of Versailles *per se* that caused renewed conflict in 1939. The key element was the arrival of Adolf Hitler in the Chancellery in Berlin at the end of January 1933. Resentment of Versailles had played a part in the complex process that brought Hitler to power but it was only one ingredient.

Hitler, however, was the vital ingredient in the outbreak of a European war in September 1939 and in the assault on France in May 1940. Historians hate being monocausal, yet it is difficult to escape being so in this case. As General Ludendorff, his erstwhile partner in the Munich Putsch of 1923 was to say of him ten years later: 'This accursed man will lead Germany into the Abyss.' Hitler made it clear from the word go that war was what he sought. Ian Kershaw writes of Hitler accepting war as a 'panacea': 'Whatever the difficulties, they would be – and could only be – resolved by war.'

In his first Cabinet meeting Hitler laid down the absolute priority of rearmament and the building of a war economy. To Hitler, war was not simply an unavoidable necessity for solving international disputes, it was desirable for its own sake. Men were fundamentally warriors, women the breeders of warriors. War kept human society healthy. It was the ultimate exercise. The Nazi regime saw its fundamental purpose in victory and conquest. The attempt was even made to condition children through nursery rhymes to love the rat-tat-tat of a machine gun. Hitler Youth training camps openly exalted war and the warrior mentality. The curriculum in schools was amended with an increased emphasis on sport, fitness and service to

Background

the Fatherland. There could be little doubt that the new Nazi Germany posed a threat to its neighbours.

In 1933 Germany left the Geneva Disarmament Conference and the League of Nations. Two years later Hitler announced the expansion of the army beyond the limits imposed by Versailles and the existence of an air force. Defence spending rose rapidly. In March 1936 Hitler took a bigger risk and remilitarised the Rhineland, gambling on French and British passivity. He was proved right and enjoyed a major triumph. In this policy the Nazi regime enjoyed widespread support and much cooperation from non-Nazi nationalists, who believed in the restoration of Germany's 'great power status' lost in 1919. Yet they did not seek war for its own sake and hoped to avoid it. As time went by and the fundamentalist nature of the regime became clearer, many nationalist fellow-travellers resigned or were dismissed, clearing the way for more extremist Nazi control. Hjalmar Schacht, the initial mastermind behind Germany's economic recovery and the initial rearmament programme, resigned in 1937 convinced that rearmament was going too far too fast. Hitler would brook no moderation in the drive towards his war economy. The conservative Foreign Minister von Neurath was replaced by the Nazi von Ribbentrop in 1938 and in the same year Hitler tightened his grip on the Army High Command, making himself Minister of Defence in place of the disgraced General Blomberg. By 1938 the special camps like Dachau, which had been nearly emptied of inmates in 1934–1935 were being refilled with opponents and potential opponents of the regime. The Nazi grip on Germany was tighter than ever.

The response of the British and French to the Nazi challenge had been mixed. There was a reluctance to resort to war and a belief, particularly in Britain, that Germany had been harshly treated in 1919 and the balm of a few concessions could reduce the Nazi inflammation. Britain agreed to sign a Treaty in 1935 allowing German naval rearmament, although limited to a maximum of 35 per cent of the British Fleet. Britain was unwilling to oppose the German reoccupation of the Rhineland in 1936 and without British support France would not act. In 1938 German troops marched into Austria in a peaceful takeover – although one forbidden under the Treaty of Versailles. Britain and France did nothing. It was, after all, a German-speaking country and the move seemed to enjoy widespread support in Austria. Britain returned to Berlin Austrian state gold deposits held in London.

Meanwhile, both the western democracies had been slow to match the German rearmament programme, largely for economic reasons. This meant that, by 1938, there was a widespread fear in both countries that German air power might be able to deal devastating blows on London and Paris. Fear now provided an additional motive for appeasing Germany. In September 1938 war seemed likely over Czechoslovakia. Germany claimed that the German-speaking minority in the borderlands were being mistreated and should be allowed to join the Reich. Hitler's motives were to destroy the whole Czech state through war, not just secure these Sudetenland Germans. Chamberlain avoided war by negotiating the transfer of the German-speaking territories to the Reich, thereby robbing the Führer of his war, much to the latter's displeasure. The crisis, however, led to a massive increase in British and French rearmament, which in a short time was likely to tilt the balance against Germany.

Hitler precipitated conflict in 1939 over Poland. He hoped to reduce Poland to subservience without a war with Britain and France but was determined this time, when Poland refused to make any concessions, to have his war. He told Germany's military leaders that if Chamberlain interfered again, as in 1938, he would kick him downstairs and jump on his belly. Britain and France were feeling more confident as a result of their rearmament programme and guaranteed the integrity of the Polish state in an attempt to warn Hitler off or at least force him to the negotiating table. Hitler was not to be warned off and when, during the August crisis, Göring suggested to his boss that it was not necessary to go for broke and some compromise settlement could be reached, Hitler famously replied: 'I've always gone for broke.' The German tanks rolled into Poland on 1 September 1939. Two days later Britain declared war, followed a few hours later by France.

The Defeat of Poland and the Phoney War

That Poland was defeated so quickly in September 1939 is not surprising. The Polish Army was outnumbered, could be assaulted from three sides and was poorly equipped by comparison with its

Background

German attackers. The Polish Air Force was overwhelmingly outnumbered and equipped with obsolescent machines. It fought bravely but was rapidly wiped out. The Poles were relying on a French offensive in the west to relieve pressure and the massively outnumbered German forces left to guard Germany's western frontier certainly feared such an attack. The Germans had no tanks available and ammunition for only three days. Halder and the General Staff felt that the French would easily reach the Rhine and threaten the industrial heart of Germany. As one future German General, then a young Major, wrote:

> Every expert serving at the time in the Western Army felt his hair stand on end when he considered the possibility of an immediate French attack.

Yet the French High Command had no plans for a major offensive. They were handicapped by Belgian neutrality, which limited the area that could be attacked to a narrow front – that which was best defended. They launched a token assault in the Saar with nine divisions and advanced 5 miles. On news of Poland's surrender, French troops withdrew to the Maginot Line. France proposed to wait for the build-up of British forces and in the meantime to prepare to withstand the inevitable German assault.

Hitler was determined to launch such an assault as soon as possible, partly for the same reasons that the French were prepared to wait. Hitler agreed with Gamelin that time was on the Allied side. British war production was accelerating rapidly. In 1940 Britain alone outproduced Germany in military aircraft by 50 per cent and, ominously, French arms production was getting into its stride. New French fighters – such as the Dewoitine D520 – were to enter service in 1940 and French tank production was approaching that of Germany in 1939. By 1940 the two western powers would easily outproduce the Third Reich in tanks – and French tanks were better. Supplies also began to pour across the Atlantic as Britain and France placed orders with the vast industrial complex that existed in the USA. In the early part of 1940 orders were placed for 10,000 military aircraft to be delivered by the end of 1941. This was the equivalent to the entire German production in a year. As early as 27 September

Dunkirk and the Fall of France

1939 Hitler was urging his military chiefs to launch an assault in the west. His Luftwaffe adjutant records him as saying:

> Time was not on our side. In six months Britain and France would be better placed than now.

Germany, by comparison, was experiencing many economic problems. The tonnage and value of German imports fell by 75 per cent. Fuel stocks fell dangerously. Supplies of gasoline fell from 300,000 tons in September 1939 to only 110,000 in April 1940. There was a major crisis over the winter months in energy supplies, as the German railway network failed to cope with the essential movement of coal.

Much is usually made of the poor morale and anti-war sentiment in France during the winter months of the so-called 'Phoney War'. In reality France was gearing itself to fight and the new ministry of armaments, under the able Raoul Dautry, was going far to sort out the hold-ups that had bedevilled French production in previous years. The production of the excellent 47mm anti-tank gun doubled between September and April, ensuring there were about 1,000 of these by May – although not all had been issued to front-line units.

The outbreak of war had not been greeted with enthusiasm but there was minimal opposition and, as in Britain, a grim determination to get it over with. In Germany the war was widely unpopular, necessitating an increase in repressive measures on behalf of Hitler's Government. And the prospect of an assault in the west led to fresh plans, among some senior military figures, of an anti-Nazi coup. Because Germany won in the summer of 1940, the fragility of German morale and the weaknesses of the German economy tend to receive little attention from historians, who focus instead on Allied weaknesses.

The German General Staff had little faith in their army's ability to crush France and were horrified at the prospect of Hitler ordering an early offensive. The conflict in Poland had revealed all manner of weaknesses, as well as leading to serious depletion of ammunition stocks and damage to aircraft and tanks, 25 per cent of which had been knocked out. Many German units had shown a lack of aggressiveness under fire and a lack of initiative in NCO and officer leadership was noted. Cooperation between Luftwaffe and ground units was often poor, with German armour suffering 'friendly' attacks by German aircraft. The German High Command required six months of training to correct defects. Hitler, however, suspected this was merely an attempt to delay an assault, and only bad weather prevented him ordering an attack: indeed, at various times in November and December, troops were ordered to jumping-off points for an attack. Only when a copy of the German plan fell into Allied hands in January did Hitler agree to a delay. It is interesting to speculate what would have been the result of a German attack in December, with Germany attacking exactly as the French anticipated and without the benefit of the new training developed as a result of deficiencies revealed in the Polish campaign. The repeated alerts also had the effect of inducing an over-relaxed attitude in the French, Belgians and Dutch to the real assault in May 1940, of which they got clear warning from anti-Nazi elements in the German military intelligence.

The Contending Armies and Their Weapons in 1940

The German Attacker
By May of 1940, Germany had assembled an army of 136 divisions in the west. The popular impression, fostered after the collapse of France, is of an overwhelmingly modern army, which completely outclassed its opponents in equipment, morale and training. Such an impression is misleading. There were ten Panzer, armoured or tank, divisions that were to form the spearhead of the attacks and these were, on the whole, very impressive. Much had been learned by the German High Command over the past two years. The peaceful occupation of Austria in March 1938 had been a shambles in terms of traffic jams and broken-down vehicles, and the importance of traffic control and road clearance and vehicle repair had been much improved since. A key element of the multi-faceted services available within the division were three mobile workshops for repair and recovery. Guderian, the father of the Panzer force, learned the importance of carrying three to five days' supplies of fuel, food and other necessaries to keep the armoured columns going, plus a large mobile supply train was included in every Panzer division. It is important to realise that a single Panzer division occupied 70 miles of

road if moving under its own power and, if moved by rail, required eighty trains of fifty-five wagons each. More had been learned in the real combat faced in Poland. The Panzer divisions of May 1940 were flexible mobile armies composed of tank battalions, motorised infantry regiments, a motorcycle battalion, an artillery regiment, signals and the combat engineers, whom the Germans referred to as pioneers. This latter group were among the most important in the division, controlling specialist equipment such as mines, flamethrowers, mine-detection equipment, inflatable boats and bridge-building materials. In the evolution of effective armoured units the German Army was certainly ahead of its opponents. Experience and experiment had taught the value of a balanced force not too heavily overladen with tanks at the expense of other arms. A Panzer division would normally have approximately 250 tanks of differing capabilities.

However, there is a grave danger in painting too rosy a picture of Germany's mastery of armoured warfare. Of the 2,439 tanks available to the German Army in the west, 523 were the light Panzer Is, already obsolete and no match for either the British or French tanks. The 955 Panzer IIs were little better with totally inadequate armour and firepower. The Germans themselves felt that only their Panzer IIIs (349) and the heavy Panzer IVs (278) were able to face those of the enemy and both were in woefully short supply. Each tank was hand built, not mass produced, and even these more modern machines lacked real hitting power. To try to make up the gap 334 Czech tanks were converted for use. In other words, one-third of the crucial German tank force was improvised from Germany's recent conquest. Nor was the doctrine of what became known as 'Blitzkrieg' fully worked out or accepted in May 1940. At one end of the spectrum was Heinz Guderian, the Commander of the biggest single Panzer components, XIX Corps, with three armoured divisions. He fully believed in the power of speed, thrust and deep penetration to destabilise an enemy. None of his superiors did, other than his ultimate superior, Hitler, and he had to believe in it out of desperation, for there was nothing else to rescue him from the hopeless strategic position into which he had led his beloved Fatherland. Rommel, the Commander of the 7th Panzer Division in Hoth's XV Panzer Corps, was new to tank warfare and saw it very

Background

much as a variant on the stormtrooper tactics of 1918. In this he was probably closer to the bulk of the senior figures within the German Army. Only after the triumph of 1940 did Blitzkrieg as a new concept become wholly accepted, forming the basis of the attack on Russia in 1941 – when, of course, it failed.

In addition, the Third Reich suffered from a fundamental economic weakness that was to bedevil its performance throughout the war. There was an acute shortage of motor vehicles and lorries in particular. The German motor industry was less developed than that of Britain and massively smaller than that of the USA. Supplies to the army proved a constant problem. In 1938 there were 100 different types of lorries in use with the army and 150 different types of motorcycle. By the middle of the war there were 151 different types of lorry and still 150 different types of motorcycle. In 1939, 16,000 civilian motors were commandeered. German production could not keep up with losses during the period of the Phoney War let alone make good the massive write off necessitated by conflict in Poland. Franz Halder, the Chief of the General Staff, recorded the worrying trend in his journal and had to contemplate a 'demotorisation' programme, by which motor vehicles were replaced by horses. Only six of the German Army's infantry divisions were motorised in May of 1940. The rest relied – as the armies of 1914–1918 or even Napoleon's had – on horses. The typical infantry division of 17,000 men required 5,375 horses, which in their turn required 53 tons of oats and hay daily.

The bulk of the German Army in 1940 was composed of such divisions. They were of vastly varying quality. Forty-six were 'first wave' divisions, composed of well-trained regulars for the most part. Each man had a conventional bolt-action rifle but the availability of other weapons gave German infantry flexibility and punch. Each ten-man rifle squad had one of the new light machine guns, the MG34. This weighed only 25 pounds compared to the old water-cooled machine gun of World War One, with its three-man team and weight of 125 pounds. Each platoon had a 50mm mortar. A heavier weapons support company in each battalion gave greater firepower in terms of anti-tank and anti-aircraft guns. Divisional artillery provided really heavy support. The combat effectiveness of the best German units came from intensive training, flexibility in weapon use and a command doctrine that emphasised individual initiative down to NCO level. In this, German units showed a marked superiority to their British and French opponents, who tended to have a more rigid and prescriptive approach. The loss of officers could induce paralysis in the Allied armies. This did not tend to happen in the first wave formations of the German Army. However, large numbers of the German infantry units were not 'first-wave' and were relatively newly raised and did not inspire the German High Command with confidence. Certainly they felt that the forces available were inferior to the old Imperial German Army that had invaded France in 1914 and failed. Even the best infantry divisions were going to find it impossible to keep up with the Panzers, a problem that had been clearly identified in the Polish campaign. The possibility of a dangerous gap opening between the armoured spearhead and the follow-up infantry was to be a constant worry to the entire German command structure from Hitler down.

Who was in control is not an easy question to answer. Nazi Germany was, in theory, a dictatorship, and certainly Hitler exercised considerable powers. Since 1938 he had been Minister of Defence and since 1934 head of state, to whom all army officers swore an oath of loyalty. His powers were considerable but he was in awe of the senior officer corps, whose professionalism he respected, even if at times he railed against them. At the top of the army was von Brauchitsch, appointed in 1938 as Commander-in-Chief in place of the disgraced Fritsch, a much more assertive character. Brauchitsch was largely responsible for the development of the 88mm dual-purpose anti-aircraft and anti-tank gun, and was a thoroughly competent professional, but he owed Hitler a personal debt of gratitude for the grant of 80,000 marks that made his divorce and remarriage possible. His influence on the 1940 campaign was minimal. Von Rundstedt, Commander of the key Army Group A, was an elderly professional, already sixty-five years old in 1940. He was widely respected within the army and although privately anti-Nazi, like so many senior officers, felt that the army should keep out of politics. Hitler appreciated his talents and beliefs and cultivated him. Although he commanded the army group that made the crucial breakthrough, it is doubtful that he grasped the concept of Blitzkrieg as preached by his subordinate, Guderian. At one stage he suggested holding back the Panzers to allow the infantry to make the initial crossing of the Meuse. Franz von Halder, the Chief of the General Staff, was one of the other key decision makers and even more anti-Nazi than von Rundstedt. Like him he was initially dubious about the concept of Blitzkrieg but his professionalism and attention to detail was vital in translating the concepts of von Manstein (von Rundstedt's Chief of Staff in 1939) and Guderian into a workable plan. Germany in 1940 had an impressive team, headed by the impressionistic and creative Hitler, but backed up by a large number of hardbitten professionals able to translate concepts into military action.

The Defenders – The French

A vital element in French defence planning was, of course, the infamous line of fortifications built along France's eastern border with Germany and named after the then minister of defence, M. Maginot. Work had started in 1930 and was largely finished by 1934 but additions were added up to 1937. It is often wrongly seen as being at the root of France's problems in 1940 or at best as a white elephant. Many have written about it as a mental and moral disaster, inducing complacency and a totally defensive attitude in both French society and military planners. In fact it was a brilliant feat of engineering with its underground power stations, hospitals, cinemas and railway. Its heavy gun emplacements posed a formidable barrier to any would-be attacker – that is, Germany. Its purpose, however, was to release sufficient troops for a forward move into Belgium to meet the aggressor there, and from Belgium to advance by the easiest route into the economic heartland of the Third Reich. It was, in other words, an intelligent answer to the problem facing French planners of a much larger German population from which a much larger army could be raised. The big hitch arose in 1936 when Belgium announced its neutrality and thus called into question a key part of French strategy. Gamelin now placed his hopes that in the event of war the Belgians would resume friendly cooperation and in the meantime unofficial links were maintained with the Belgian High Command.

By 1940 France had been able to mobilise ninety-four divisions for service in the home country: three facing the Italians on the Alpine frontier and the rest available against the Germans. Thirteen were fortification troops mainly manning the Maginot Line. There were five cavalry divisions, partly mechanised; three new heavy armoured divisions; three light mechanised divisions and seven motorised infantry divisions – one more than in the German Army. France had not neglected tank design and by 1940 had what were generally considered the best two in service anywhere. There were the 260 SOMUA S35s with a powerful gun, adequate armour and a good turn of speed. It was generally considered the best tank in Europe. In addition there were 311 Char B1 *bis* heavy tanks with a steering system ahead of anything in the German Army and over much of its armour, impervious to German tank shells. With older tanks France outnumbered Germany, although many lacked radios and there were weaknesses in terms of the manning and control. France was behind Germany in the organisation of armoured divisions. The light mechanised divisions, DLMs, were most like the German Panzers with approximately 200 tanks, motorised infantry battalions, artillery, engineers and motorcycle units. They were a balanced modern fighting force. It was only in the aftermath of the collapse of Poland that the French High Command began to organise three heavy tank divisions known as DCRs. They were smaller than the DLMs with only 156 tanks and only one battalion of motorised infantry attached and no motorcycles. They had not really had time to evolve into the balanced force they needed to be to counter the more experienced Panzers, and by May only the 1st and 2nd DCRs were up to strength. The majority of French tanks were scattered amongst the infantry divisions as support, in the manner of the First World War.

The sixty-three infantry divisions that were not motorised resembled those of the German Army. Thirty were regular divisions composed of fit and well trained men. Many had had combat experience in the colonies. The class A reserve divisions were also of reasonable quality. The problems occurred with the class B reserves, who were older, often in their thirties, with reservist officers and NCOs and old equipment. The key point of impact of the German attack struck, by chance, the class B 55th Infantry Division at Sedan, and there was one other B Division in Huntzinger's Second Army. Likewise, in Corap's Ninth Army to the north there were two B

Background

divisions, also in the line of the Panzer assault in May. Elsewhere French infantry fought ferociously and on the Alpine Front three French divisions held off an Italian force of seven times their strength, which also enjoyed overwhelming air support. The German Army also had its B divisions, many in Army Group C, under General von Leeb, facing the Maginot Line. These were popularly referred to in the German Army as 'von Leeb's Museum'. The equipment of the French Army was not markedly inferior to that in the German. Tanks have already been referred to. Certain weapons, such as anti-tank guns, were still in short supply but this was improving rapidly by May. In artillery the French had an overwhelming superiority with 10,700 to 7,378, although many of the French guns were the 75mm of 1914–1918 vintage. The reliance on horsepower, as in the bulk of the German Army, limited the mobility of much of the French artillery.

The German planners had respect for the intelligence and competence of the French General Staff, which they recognised as thoroughly professional, but they identified key weaknesses in the whole command structure of the French Army. It was methodical to a fault, with detailed orders for every situation envisaged. Individual initiative was not encouraged as in the German Army. Gamelin distrusted radio and telephone communication fearing, quite rightly, that lines could be intercepted and decrypted, as the French were effectively doing to German communications traffic. To ensure security, which became a French obsession, Gamelin relied on motorcycle couriers. This combined with the clumsy command structure (see glossary in the Appendices) ensured that decisions were made and passed on at the speed of 1918, not as they should have been in 1940. Much is often made of the supposed contrast between the rigorous training the German Army underwent during the period of the Phoney War and the time wasted by the French and the consequent deterioration in morale. Such a comparison is unfair. Giraud's Seventh Army on the extreme west of the French line undertook exhaustive training in terrain similar to that north of Antwerp, where they were scheduled to engage the enemy, and the two DLMs under General Prioux practised engagements in territory similar to the Gembloux Gap, which was their destination. All in all, the French Army of 1940 appeared to have a good chance of holding and repulsing a German attack, even if much ground had to be surrendered as in 1918. Both Stalin and Churchill had great faith in the French Army and expected it ultimately to prevail, as the British contribution expanded and the superior economic resources of the Allies could be brought to bear.

The Defenders – The British Field Force

By comparison with its French allies and German enemies the British Field Force was tiny and under-prepared. By May 1940 there were ten infantry divisions facing the Germans. Five of them were composed of regulars and these had been efficiently dispatched in 1939. A further five Territorial divisions were dispatched in 1940 and each contained a stiffening of one regular battalion in each brigade. The Territorials in particular suffered from a shortage of experienced officers and NCOs. All ten divisions were intended to be motorised and there was enough transport for supplies and equipment, if not for all the troops. Many civilian lorries had been pressed into service, as in the German Army, and Major General Montgomery, Commander of the 3rd Division, complained bitterly of their unreliability. In addition there were a further three Territorial divisions available for labour and supplies but these were quite untrained and ill-equipped for fighting. There were two reconnaissance tank brigades with light tanks and an army tank brigade, composed of the ponderous Matilda infantry tanks. These were so heavily armoured that they were invulnerable to most German firepower but they were slow and prone to breakdown. A new armoured division was forming in England with 312 cruiser tanks and two motorised rifle battalions of high quality.

The Field Force reflected its hasty, recent creation and the long years of neglect from which the army had suffered. Priority in spending had gone to the navy and particularly the air force, and it had only been in February 1939 that the UK Government had accepted the need for an 'effort of blood' as the French termed it. The army would need time to regain its skills. The equipment was steadily improving in 1940 but the army was being trained to replay its role of 1917–1918, that is holding the front. The basic infantry weapon was the Lee-Enfield .303 and the increasingly available light machine gun, the Bren. Both weapons went right through the war, proving

Background

robust and serviceable. Increasing numbers of mortars were available and the anti-tank platoon of the battalion had the excellent (for its time) 2-pounder anti-tank gun. Anti-tank rifles, which were also provided for infantry defence against tanks, were less well loved with good reason: they were largely ineffective. The army of 1940 had a considerably longer logistical and support tail than armies of the past. Far larger numbers served in one of the many servicing corps essential for modern warfare. Churchill always found this hard to accept and felt that the fighting component should be larger.

The quality of the senior commanders certainly varied. Possibly the least suitable for the job he held was John Standish Surtees Prendergast Vereker, sixth Viscount Gort. Personally brave to an almost superhuman extent and anxious for action, he was too obsessed with trivia to be an effective commander-in-chief. He frequently appalled his senior colleagues by giving priority to such vital issues as to whether the tin hat, when off a soldier's head should be carried on the left or right shoulder. His two leading subordinates commanding the two initial army corps were both able and intelligent soldiers, Sir Alan Brooke and Sir John Dill. At divisional level were Major-Generals Bernard Montgomery, in charge of the 3rd, and Harold Alexander, in command of the 1st. The latter was to earn distinction as Commander of the Dunkirk perimeter in early June. The German assessments, before May, of the British forces was complimentary regarding their tenacity in defence, drawing attention to the British capacity for 'self-sacrifice, bravery, and strong nerves in the face of setbacks'. On the other hand, the Germans reckoned that British Army leadership was 'in general schematic and slow'. The same report went on: 'In the lower ranks limited independence in decision is particularly apparent.' In many ways such criticism was accurate and appropriate throughout the entire war, not just in 1940.

The Defenders – The Belgians and the Dutch

In size the Belgian Army was a formidable addition to the Allied cause. There were twenty-two divisions by May of 1940 composed of eighteen infantry divisions, two divisions of Chasseurs Ardennais and two motorised cavalry divisions, 600,000 in all. Its equipment, however, left much to be desired. There were only ten tanks and no anti-aircraft guns. It was very much an army of 1918 and well capable of stubborn bravery in defence. Like France, much had been spent on static defence positions, such as the formidable fort of Eben Emael, guarding the Albert Canal crossings north of Liège. The army had suffered from the declaration of neutrality in 1936 and the breakdown of coordination with the French Army. Nevertheless, despite its shortcomings, the Belgian Army could prove a tough opponent, as the official history of the German 12th Division spoke of the 'extraordinary bravery of its soldiers'.

The Dutch Army was smaller with ten to eleven divisions or their equivalents and handicapped by the small size of the area to be defended. It was only 60 miles from the German border to the heart of Fortress Holland. The best troops were in the Dutch East Indies. Most of the army available to defend the homeland were reservists and required time to reach their units. By then, much of the Netherlands was likely to be occupied. There had been a strong pacifist tradition in the country and much opposition to military expenditure. The result of this was that the Dutch Army had only twenty-six armoured cars, no tanks and 656 old-fashioned pieces of artillery. The rapid defeat and occupation of the Netherlands is a terrible warning against seeing the world as you would have it, as opposed to how it is.

Air Power

Air power was to play a crucial and almost decisive part in the rapid defeat of both the Netherlands and Belgium. Estimates vary as to the numbers the Luftwaffe was able to deploy in May 1940. The total in all theatres was over 1,700 fighters and over 2,100 bombers and a substantial force of transport and reconnaissance planes. Supporting the western attack in May were around 1,600 bombers, including approximately 400 dive-bombers. These were protected by 1,220 fighters. Opposing the German forces was a much smaller number of Allied bombers, 377 (British and French planes) and 898 Allied fighters (not including the Dutch and Belgian planes). There was clearly an advantage to the Germans in numbers and this was enhanced by, on the whole, having superior planes and a more developed doctrine of close aerial support.

On several occasions it was attack by the fearsome Junkers 87 dive-bomber or Stuka that had a devastating effect. French horse-

Background

drawn artillery were particularly vulnerable. The plane itself was not new and very vulnerable to fighter attack and effective anti-aircraft fire. On one occasion twelve Ju 87s were shot down by five French fighters for no fighter loss. Unfortunately, the Germans usually escorted their Stukas for the most part, and both the French and British were deficient in anti-aircraft guns. The German Air Force had a long tradition of cooperation with the army, going back to the First World War, and this had been enhanced by their experiences in the Spanish Civil War, when the German Condor Legion had been able to acquire vital practice. This had been further polished up in the short campaign in Poland. In addition, Junkers 52 transport planes were to play a key role in keeping the momentum of armoured warfare going. The Luftwaffe was to show great enterprise in moving forward rapidly behind the advancing tanks and establishing forward bases. The basic German fighter, the Messerschmitt 109 E, was excellent if difficult to fly and superior to most French fighters. For all their advantages, however, one recent study has concluded:

> the German Air Force was proved weak in a multitude of ways, and, other than in the application of air resources in certain areas and circumstances, the Luftwaffe was only moderately better prepared for the style of campaign in France than its adversaries.

It was in close air support that the Allies were most deficient. The RAF was a formidable force but had focused on strategic bombing and the air defence of the UK. It had early on established its independence from the army and was deeply suspicious of army control. A force of light bombers, composed of Blenheims and Fairey Battles, was dispatched to France but the latter were almost obsolete and suffered a horrendous attrition rate, which was testament to the bravery of the pilots and the inadequacies of the machines. Four squadrons of Hurricane fighters were initially sent out, and although slower than the Messerschmitt, were tough and easy to fly. They performed well. The squadrons of the more modern Spitfire were retained in Britain. The most common French fighter was the Moraine–Saullnier, an early monoplane but already obsolete by 1940 and being replaced by the newer Dewoitine D520 and Bloch MB152. In the meantime, the

French were taking delivery of the Curtiss Hawk 75. This, in theory, was inferior to the Me 109 but in practice gave a very good account of itself. In November of 1939 a whole Gruppe of Me 109 Ds, outnumbering nine Hawks by three-to-one, were thrashed with four 109s shot down and four more damaged for the loss of only one Curtiss Hawk, which belly-landed with an unhurt pilot.

In fact the skill and professionalism of the French Air Force was high, as the casualties inflicted on the Luftwaffe indicates. With the Allies expanding production of new and superior aircraft, the German advantage in air power was likely to diminish rapidly in the course of 1940. In May, however, it still had the edge.

Plans and Intelligence Gathering

The Evolution of 'Sichelschnitt'

The drive and impetus to attack France and the Low Countries came from Hitler alone. On 27 September, even before the Poles finally surrendered, he told General Halder to prepare an assault on France, Belgium and Holland. He was contemptuous of the French, according to Halder:

> The French will not have the stuff of the Poles [...] The decisive element will be the English.

Hitler wanted as much of Belgium, Holland and northern France occupied as possible, in order to push the war against the United Kingdom. He wanted an attack by the end of October. Halder and Brauchitsch were horrified. They felt that an attack stood no hope of success and began to talk of the need for 'fundamental changes' – that is a military coup to remove Hitler and the Nazi regime. There were many, in particular inside the Abwehr (German military intelligence), who supported such action. The senior officers – Generals von Bock, von Leeb and von Kluge – responsible for executing any attack on France agreed with the General Staff that a successful attack was out of the question. Even the pro-Nazi Reichanau agreed with von Bock, his superior, on the lack of feasibility in 1939. Hitler insisted on 17 October that an attack should go ahead on 12 November.

Background

With the greatest reluctance, and with no belief in success, the General Staff came up with Case Yellow – in effect, a replay of the Schlieffen Plan of 1914. Basic geography dictated much of the planning and the Maginot Line further limited the options. The easiest approach to northern France and Paris was through Belgium, using the so-called Gembloux Gap between Namur and Wavre for the central thrust. It was presented to Hitler on 25 October. Its presenters showed little enthusiasm and Hitler received it with little. The main thrust would be carried out by von Bock's Army Group, which would contain the bulk of the Panzer divisions. To the south, facing Luxembourg, a second Army Group, under von Rundstedt, would adopt a defensive role, guarding the flanks of the main thrust. A third Army Group in the extreme south, facing the Maginot Line, under von Leeb, would try to fix as many enemy forces as possible there. A second variant of the plan at the end of October involved ignoring Holland altogether. To this the Luftwaffe objected on the grounds that they needed the Dutch coast for operations against England. The Eighteenth Army, with only one weak Panzer division but with a very strong air component, was set aside for the seizure of the Netherlands. There were also increasing objections from von Rundstedt and his brilliant and assertive Chief of Staff, von Manstein, who argued for the need to be flexible and exploit opportunities in the south around Sedan, should they occur. Von Manstein argued that the existing Case Yellow only offered an improved position, not victory. He argued that if the main thrust was through the Ardennes towards Sedan, real surprise could be achieved and a decisive victory gained. The Ardennes, with its heavily wooded hills and narrow meandering valleys through which the roads ran, was thought largely impassable for a major offensive force. Von Manstein consulted Guderian, who agreed that with detailed planning and some luck, sufficient forces could be passed through the region to reach the Meuse at Sedan within three days. The General Staff disagreed and some war games as late as February 1940 suggested it could take nine. Halder personally disliked von Manstein, and Brauchitsch disliked von Rundstedt, and they saw their suggestions simply as jealous attempts to boost their importance at the expense of Bock. Hitler, however, was unhappy with the plan and in November, as the date for the launch of the offensive was postponed time after time, a 'play it by ear' plan evolved. Von Rundstedt received four Panzer divisions and two of motorised infantry, with the option of exploiting any weakness on his front. Bock, however, still had the majority of the Panzers and would make the main thrust or *Schwerpunkt*. Hitler still demanded an early attack and after poor weather in December enforced yet another delay, it was decided that a cold clear January would be suitable for the execution of this modified Case Yellow. Chance intervened.

By mid December von Manstein had gone beyond recommending flexibility and the option of a secondary thrust through the Ardennes, and in a memo of 18 December argued for transferring the primary thrust to Rundstedt's force. Just before this, Halder had decided to get the irritating von Manstein out of the way and promote him to the command of a corps in Poland. When he received von Manstein's proposal on 19 December Halder referred to it as 'idiotic'. However, over the next few weeks he became more and more convinced of its virtues. Part of the process was a series of war games played by the General Staff intelligence analysts. These suggested that a thrust through the Ardennes could work largely as a result of the slow reaction time of the French General Staff and as long as they could be fooled into believing the main thrust was in the north, towards Brussels. It was two accidents that completed the evolution of the Sickle Cut plan of May. First, on 10 January 1940, just before the latest launch date for the attack, a German plane flying to Cologne strayed over the Belgian border and crash-landed near Mechelen. The German officers on board were carrying many details relating to the plan of attack. The result was that it was postponed once more, till spring, and subjected to major alteration. The other chance influence was that von Manstein secured an interview with Hitler as he was being transferred to Poland and convinced the dictator of the correctness of making the Ardennes offensive the main one. In one sense he was pushing at an open door, in that Hitler was less than enthusiastic about the original Case Yellow and was attracted by the possibilities of the decisive result offered by von Manstein. Over the next two months the final German plan emerged. The key point of the attack would be headed by seven Panzer divisions within Army Group A, under von Rundstedt's command. A major secondary attack would still be necessary in the north by Bock's Army Group B to fix the attention of the French and British. There were last-minute hitches as Rundstedt and his new chief of staff began to doubt the feasibility of making the breakthrough on the Meuse with the Panzer divisions and proposed to substitute an infantry attack. This would have fatally slowed the time required to cover the 85 miles from the German border to the Meuse and even Halder backed Guderian in stressing that time was of the essence to prevent the French realising they had been fooled and shifting forces back to the *Schwerpunkt* at Sedan and Dinant. Such debates indicate that the concept of Blitzkrieg – so often ascribed to the plan – was not fully worked out. The final plan was the result not of some underpinning concept but the complex interplay of personalities and luck. Halder gave it a one-in-ten chance of success.

French Planning – The Dyle Plan

French planning was not idiotic as is so often believed today. It reflected the views of intelligent professionals using the information available to them in the light of their experience. The basic assumptions made by Gamelin and his Staff were remarkably similar to those of the German General Staff. It was a combination of a talented amateur, Adolf Hitler, luck, the Mechelen plane crash, and the partly self-interested genius of von Manstein that negated the assumptions of the two General Staffs.

Gamelin and his Staff considered the Ardennes as a point of attack and decided that it would take nine or ten days to pass sufficient forces through them to have any chance of success. Such a time would always provide the option of reinforcing any threatened point, such as Sedan. Far more likely as providing appropriate terrain for tank attacks were the flat plains of Belgium and in particular the Gembloux Gap. On the Belgian border, Gamelin placed his best and most mobile troops under Blanchard. It contained two of France's excellent light mechanised divisions and three motorised divisions. Ideally, a coordinated policy with the Belgian Government should be worked out but Belgian neutrality prevented this. The safe option – and the one favoured by Gamelin's chief subordinate, General Georges, Commander of the north-eastern front – was the Escaut Line. This involved sticking to the prepared positions along the French–Belgian border, from just north-east of Sedan to Lille, and then advancing into Belgium in the coastal west of the country and defending along the line of the Scheldt and Escaut from Antwerp to Lille. This meant abandoning Brussels and much of Belgium to the German invaders. The alternative plan was to advance further into Belgium and occupy the line of the Dyle river from Antwerp to Wavre and then hold the Gembloux Gap to Namur and thence down the Meuse to Sedan. The difficulty was the advance without previous preparation and the absence for 25 miles of a river line from Wavre to Namur. The advantages were considerable, as it involved a 50-mile shortening of the front to be held and the holding of much of Belgium's industrial areas, including Brussels. Gamelin was persuaded to adopt this D (Dyle) Plan in the autumn of 1939, when he was led to believe that the Belgians were effectively fortifying the Gembloux Gap and Lord Gort of the BEF approved of the advance (Gort tended to approve of anything suggested by the French senior Staff). The Dyle Plan, although posing some problems, did make sense, and fitted with the cautious approach of the methodical Gamelin. However, quite incautiously in March 1940, Gamelin decided to graft onto the Dyle Plan, what was known as the Breda variant. This involved a dash up the Belgian coast by the mobile Seventh Army, under General Giraud, to north of Antwerp to link with the Dutch, in the hope of keeping them in the war. It was a sign of confidence on Gamelin's part and rather uncharacteristically risky. News of this to the Germans, via decrypts, convinced them that their Sickle Cut had a better chance. Gamelin was going to use the best part of the French reserves under General Giraud to make the Breda dash. Giraud, himself and General Georges were deeply sceptical. It was a serious mistake.

Campaign Chronicle

⬤

10 May: The Assault on the Netherlands
The Dutch had advanced warning of the attack from Colonel Hans Oster of the Abwehr, a brave and persistent anti-Nazi who had developed a close relationship with the Dutch Military Attaché, Major Sas, in Berlin. He had already been the recipient of a whole series of warnings since November 1939, as Hitler struggled to get an attack launched and faced repeated problems and resistance leading to cancellations. This of course weakened the impact of Sas's warnings on the night of 9 May. Sas got through to the Defence Ministry in the Hague and delivered his news. He was infuriated to receive a telephone call an hour later questioning the likelihood of the impending attack.

The Dutch defence strategy rested on trying to hold the frontier on the River Maas for a time before falling back 10 miles to another temporary halt line along the River Raam in the Peel region. Finally it was hoped that Vesting Holland, Fortress Holland, could be held till relief arrived. This, utilising water obstacles (enhanced by deliberate flooding) and blockhouses, protected the capital, the Hague, and the great cities of Amsterdam and Rotterdam. Time would be necessary for the reservists to report for duty. The Germans, appreciating this and the difficulties of successive water barriers, proposed to rely on speed, air power and guile. The main thrust would be by the Austrian 9th Panzer Division supported by a division of motorised SS infantry, south of the main rivers of the Netherlands and towards Tilburg and Breda. Subordinate attacks by infantry would take place into the northern frontier provinces of Groningen and Friesland. But the key would be a series of risky airdrops into Fortress Holland itself.

Dunkirk and the Fall of France

At 3am the Dutch finally accepted the warning as genuine and began to blow the Maas bridges. The Germans tried to seize the bridges by resorting to tricks of impersonation. At Maastricht this failed but notably at Gennep, further north, they succeeded in preventing this crucial railway bridge being blown. Helped by Dutch fascist sympathisers and pretending to escort German prisoners, a small force stopped the detonation of charges and enabled an armoured German train to roll across the river, followed by another troop train. Disaster had occurred by 4am as these were able to penetrate 10 miles and pierce the Peel Line, the blockhouses of which could then be assaulted from the rear. The 9th Panzer Division was then able to cross with supporting infantry. By the end of Friday the 10th, the Maas Line had fallen as Dutch troops pulled back to the already threatened Peel Line. To the north, the Germans advanced rapidly through Groningen and Friesland to the eastern end of the great dike on the northern edge of the IJsselmeer (Zuider Zee) and were then held by fortifications as intended. Others advancing through Arnhem, after a successful paradrop there, were held on the River Lek, the eastern defence of Fortress Holland.

Air power was to deliver the most devastating blows. At 3.30am most of the airfields in Holland were bombed, including Schipol, destroying much of the small Dutch Air Force. Most of Germany's airborne troops, under Lieutenant-General Kurt Student, were now thrown into a desperate attempt to seize the Hague and Rotterdam. There were nearly 4,000 paratroopers and 12,000 specially trained airborne infantry packed into Junkers 52 transport planes. The long bridges at Moerdijk, 16 miles south of Rotterdam, were seized at 6.40am by drops to the north and south by 700 paratroopers. The same success was met with at Dordrecht, even closer to the great port city. Rotterdam's airport of Waalhaven was seized and at 7am Ju 52s began landing. One of the most extraordinary moves by the invaders was the landing of twelve seaplanes on the Nieuwe Maas in the heart of the city at 5am. They promptly seized the Willems Bridge. More paratroopers landed into a sports stadium south of this initial invasion and then joined their comrades on the bridges after commandeering tramcars and driving them through the southern city. A fierce fight developed at the northern end of the bridge as Dutch infantry counter-attacked, but the Dutch could not stop the Germans gradually flying in more men and occupying the southern part of Rotterdam. Dutch ships joined in the attacks and in the afternoon a Dutch destroyer, *Van Galen*, began shelling the airport at Waalhaven. She was eventually sunk by German bombers. Dutch and British air raids were made on Waalhaven, which was also continuously shelled by artillery from the other side of the river.

The attempt to seize the capital, the Hague, went even more seriously wrong and eventually had to be abandoned. The invaders aimed to seize three airports. Some 120 paratroopers landed at Valkenburg at first light and drove off the defending troops, but many of the heavily laden Ju 52s, flying in reinforcements, bogged down on the soft runways blocking further landings. Twenty-six aircraft tried to land on a nearby beach but many were wrecked and others strafed by the Dutch Air Force. By evening the Dutch had recaptured Valkenburg and driven the German survivors into defensive pockets. The drop on Ockenburg airfield was a disaster, with most of the paratroopers missing their drop-zone. The flat airfields were easy to miss in the early half-light. Many were captured and others forced to hide. The attack on the third airfield of Ypenburg, east of the capital, went little better. Paratroopers were scattered and Junkers 52s, landing reinforcements, were shot up and wrecked. At 5pm a squadron of British Hurricanes intervened, mainly shooting up wrecked German aircraft. By 7.30pm the commander designated to capture the Hague – and who had himself had to land in a field – admitted failure to German Headquarters and was ordered to abandon his task and try to help the small band of German troops holding on at the northern end of the Willems Bridge in Rotterdam. All was now going to turn on the struggle for this great Dutch port and city.

10 May: The Assault on Belgium

Although the thrust through Belgium was not the vital point of attack or *Schwerpunkt*, it had to be sufficiently threatening to convince the French that it was. Von Bock's Army Group B contained three Panzer divisions. The weakest was involved in the dash through southern Holland to link with the airborne attack. Two others, under General Höpner, would form the spearhead of Bock's thrust, making for the crucial Gembloux Gap, where the French expected them. The initial

German objective was crossing the Meuse (Maas) and the adjoining Albert Canal. The key points were the bridge in the Dutch city of Maastricht, the bridges over the Albert Canal and the great Belgian fort of Eben Emael to the south of Maastricht, guarding a crucial crossing. The fort had been built in 1932 to prevent an easy repeat of 1914. It was generally regarded as a piece of formidable modern engineering. Shaped like a wedge, it measured 900 yards by 770 and it took twenty minutes to walk from the main entrance to the furthest gun batteries within the fort. It had two huge 120mm guns and several 75mm, as well as machine guns and 60mm anti-tank guns covering the approaches. Hitler took it sufficiently seriously as an obstacle to devote considerable amounts of his own time to the problem of its capture. Accurate scale models were made and much research carried out as to how to take it. A special unit was trained to land by glider on the roof of the fortress at first light, others were to land near the Albert Canal bridges at the same time. The whole operation was timed to be three hours before any official declaration of war.

A combination of circumstances aided the Germans, not least the number of false alerts over the past few months. The Dutch had passed on the warnings from Sas on the evening of the 9th and various other indications of action were being gathered by Belgian Intelligence but in January, the prompt Belgian response to warnings of an impending invasion had cost the then Belgian Army Chief his job, when it turned into a false alarm. His successor was thus understandably inclined to be cautious in responding to the warnings that were flooding in on the 9th. It was not until 1.30am Belgian time that full alert was put out to the entire Belgian Army. The garrison at Eben Emael was composed of second rate and inexperienced troops and the gun that was to be fired as a warning to get men to move rapidly to combat positions was out of order and needed an hour to repair. In addition and affecting the whole Belgian Army's response to the alert was the announcement on the 9th that leave was to be increased from two to five days a month. Large numbers of officers and men concluded that the alert in the early hours of the 10th could hardly be genuine, coming just after the announcement of increased leave.

The German attacks achieved their objectives for the most part. The bridge nearest the fortress was blown before paratroopers could reach it, but the two others at Veldwezelt and Vroenhoven, just to the north, were successfully seized intact. In the case of the latter, a quick-thinking and quick-moving German paratrooper was able to extinguish the lit fuse before it detonated the charge under the bridge. At the other, the Belgian defenders were handicapped by having no primed grenades, leaving much of their ammunition in lorries too far away from their defensive positions and finding that many of their weapons refused to fire. It was a dismal saga for the defenders and a triumph for the dawn invaders. By 8.45pm the Germans had relieved the paratroopers on the bridges and sent them back to Maastricht to recuperate.

Nine gliders landed on the roof of the fortress itself. Luckily for them only one of the machine-gun positions capable of firing onto the roof was manned at the time but opted not to fire at the first glider down. The invaders immediately attacked one of the casements of the big guns. A hollow charge was used, which blasted a hole in the casement, causing devastation to the Belgians underneath. Each casement was sealed from the rest of the fortress by steel doors but the Germans tossed grenades down the shaft. Other casements were captured but not all the guns facing the Albert Canal bridges were knocked out. The garrison seems to have made no real attempt to recapture the roof and attempts by neighbouring Belgian units at 12.30 and 5pm were driven off. The fort had not been captured but partially deactivated. German troops crossed the Albert Canal in rubber boats after darkness fell and preparations were made to ensure the surrender of the fort next day.

To the south, the German invasion triggered the Allied advance into Belgium under the Dyle Plan. It was 6.50am before the Belgians invited British and French assistance. The Light Mechanised Corps, under General Prioux, composed of two DLMs, moved over the frontier at noon towards the Gembloux Gap to cover the advance of General Blanchard's First Army. Gort's British Army began to move about 1pm, its advance led by armoured cars of the 12th Lancers. The front assigned to it ran from Louvain to Wavre, which was to be held by three British divisions. Five others were to be in support. The Commander of II Corps, Lieutenant-General Alan Brooke, recorded in his diary that night:

Everything so far has been running like clockwork and with less interference from bombing than I anticipated – 3rd Division started off at 2.30pm this afternoon and by now its advance elements should be approaching the Dyle.

German air interference was of course deliberately minimal, as the charge into Belgium was just what their plan required. Near the coast, Giraud's Seventh Army began its advance to aid the Dutch, its lead elements crossing into Belgium at 10am. Most of the force was not, however, on the move till late afternoon.

10 May: The Assault on Luxembourg and the Passage Through the Ardennes

At 4.35am elements of the 1st Panzer Division crossed the Sauer river and entered Luxembourg. It was one of three Panzer divisions under the command of Hurrying Heinz Guderian, the father of German tank warfare. Guderian hoped to reach the Meuse at Sedan, 85 miles away to the west, in three days. To the north of Luxembourg two more Panzer divisions, under General Reinhardt, faced a longer and even more difficult journey, largely through Belgium, but facing the same difficult terrain of the wooded Ardennes. Small winding roads followed the sinuous valleys. Along these, Reinhardt would have to push his Panzers down to the Meuse at Montherme in France. The most northerly of the Panzer force, under Hoth, also had two Panzer divisions, one of these was the 7th under Rommel. In many ways these had the easiest journey to make, aiming to reach and cross the Belgian Meuse at Dinant, south of Namur. Hoth's Corps was to protect the flank of the true *Schwerpunkt*, making for Sedan. Rommel, however, was not the man to take a subsidiary role and he had a drive and energy to match Guderian.

Initially, the major problem was traffic control. The 'greatest traffic jam known up to that date in Europe' was being enacted by the German Army and it was highly vulnerable to air attack. An officer in the 1st Panzer Division recalled stopping at a major road junction in Diekirch:

Again and again I looked with anxious eyes at the beaming blue sky; for what a target the Division offers as long as it is compelled to progress by moving slowly forward along a single road. But not once does one French observation plane appear.

Still less were there any harassing attacks by Allied bombers or fighters. The bulk of the Allied Air Forces was engaged in covering the advance into Belgium of the BEF and Blanchard's 1st Army.

The 1st Panzer Division crossed into Belgium from Luxembourg at Martelange and here encountered resistance for the first time. The opponents were the 4th Company of the Chasseurs Ardennais. There were further delays at Bodange by the 5th Company. Fierce resistance, minefields and demolitions held the division up for eight hours and showed what might have been accomplished. The Belgians, however, retired north before being replaced by advanced forces of the French Ninth Army's cavalry – another sign of ineffective inter-Allied cooperation. The 10th Panzer Division, moving by the most southerly route, ran into light French scouting forces from Huntzinger's 2nd Army at Etalle and lost two senior regimental officers in the fighting – indicative of the German tradition of leading from the front. The most northerly of Guderian's forces, the 2nd Panzer, was the slowest, with a series of S-bends in northern Luxembourg to navigate. This force also found that the 1st Division had highjacked one of the roads dedicated to the use of the 2nd. The result was the division did not reach Belgium till the 11th. It was conflicts over road use like this that led Kleist, Guderian's superior, to threaten to shoot any officer using the wrong road.

Friday, 10 May had been a day of clear blue skies – a portent of the luck the Germans were going to enjoy with the weather and in other respects for the next few weeks. Perhaps the only ominous development for Germany was the appointment in London on this day of the 64-year-old Winston Churchill as British Prime Minister.

11–12 May: The Battle for Rotterdam and the Netherlands

Throughout Saturday fighting continued in and around Rotterdam. Vastly outnumbered, those troops who had landed to the north of the city fought desperate defensive actions to avoid capture. This was particularly hard on the Dutch inhabitants of Valkenburg, where the German paratroopers had retired to and now faced shelling from surrounding Dutch infantry. In Rotterdam the airborne attackers stubbornly tried to enlarge their hold but most of the city remained in Dutch hands. The key lay in the progress of the 9th Panzer Division under Dr Ritter von Hubicki. It crossed into the Netherlands via the Gennep Bridge and raced across to Tilburg by the morning of the 12th. Contact had also been made with some of the advanced forces of Giraud's Seventh Army near Breda, and a tank battle ensued that inflicted heavy losses on the light Panzer Is and IIs of which the 9th Division was composed. The French did not press their advantage but waited for reinforcements and in the best First World War tradition, sought to seal off the Germans from the south rather than pressing on to the Moerdijk Bridge. This enabled the 9th to reach the bridge and it was then reinforced by an SS motorised division. The chances of frustrating the bold German bid to seize the Netherlands was slipping away.

11–12 May: The Matador's Cloak Continues to Attract the Bull

The invasion of Belgium has been likened to the matador's cloak that induces the bull to charge, so that as it passes it can be struck in the flank. The best part of the French and British Armies were charging – or more accurately sedately advancing – into Belgium on the 11th, whilst the matador's sword was making its way through the Ardennes. The British Field Force moved up to the Dyle Line and the biggest problem proved to be not the Germans but the Belgians. As the 3rd Division took up its position near Louvain, the local Belgian commander objected and on the 12th the British corps commander spent fruitless hours trying to get the Belgian king to resolve the problem. The French General Georges finally ordered the Belgians to move.

The British air contingent was in action on the 12th, trying to destroy the Albert Canal bridges that the Germans had seized on the 10th. One of the bridges was damaged but for the loss of several aircraft. By the end of the 12th there were only seventy-two out of the original 135 operational bombers with the British air contingent. The RAF also lost ten Hurricane fighters on the 12th. The rate of loss began to worry the Air Ministry.

By the 11th Gamelin – and even more the French Prime Minister, Paul Reynaud – were beginning to have doubts about the main point of the German attack, but Gamelin still felt that, if necessary, it would be possible to reinforce the area around Sedan. The major tank battle that began to develop in the Gembloux Gap on the 12th partially reinforced the French belief that it was the centre of the main German thrust. General Prioux's excellent Cavalry Corps (composed of two mechanised divisions) arrived in the Gembloux Gap on the 11th with express instructions to hold up the advancing Panzers till the bulk of Blanchard's Army arrived to man the Dyle Line. Prioux was appalled to find that the Belgians had not developed the anti-tank obstacles they had led the French to believe were in place. Prioux requested that the French deployment be hastened so that his holding operation should last only until the 14th, not the originally planned 15th. On the 12th the French mechanised divisions encountered the Panzers of General Höpner's Corps and the first real tank battle in history began close to the town of Hannut. Although the French divisions were referred to as 'light', their tanks were in general superior to those of the Germans. This was particularly true of the SOMUAs, which were better armed and armoured than the Panzer IIIs and massively superior to the Panzer Is and IIs. The main disadvantage of the French tanks lay in the inferiority of the air support and the fact that the turret was a one-man affair, the tank commander being obliged to control and fire himself, compared to the three-man teamwork in the better German tanks. Despite these factors, the French divisions were to give a good account of themselves over the next two days, fulfilling their task. A German captain, Ernst von Jüngenfeld, Commander of a tank company of the 35th Panzer Regiment in the 4th Panzer Division, summarised the clash of the 12th:

> [the day was] hard and bloody, many a brave *Panzermann* had to lay down his life for the Fatherland, many were wounded and a large number of our tanks was lost, in part to shells and in part to breakdowns.

This was a very different picture from the usually received one of deficient and cowardly Frenchmen failing to confront. Where the best French troops met the best German – as in this initial encounter near to Hannut – there was little to choose between the two sides.

11–12 May: The Passage Through the Ardennes to the Meuse

As the German Panzers were threading their way through the narrow valleys, two French Armies were responding. North of Sedan the responsibility belonged to General Corap's Ninth Army, whose task was to move into Belgium and guard the Meuse up to Namur, where the Meuse had its junction with the Sambre. As befitted a 'quiet' sector, the troops were not of the best and many units were under-equipped, as Corap constantly reminded HQ. Sedan itself and the section south and east to the Maginot Line fell to Huntzinger's Second Army, also somewhat neglected as a perceived quiet front. The Germans, in consequence, had a triple advantage in their choice of *Schwerpunkt*. They achieved surprise, faced second-class French units, and struck against a hinge between two armies that confused and slowed the French responses. In addition, the section of the line given to Corap had been held by the Belgian Army until the 10th and as elsewhere, precious little cooperation had taken place. Corap was surprised by the withdrawal of the Belgian Chasseurs Ardennais to Namur on the 10th. He sent out a cavalry screen east of the Meuse to delay the advancing Germans and to link with a similar screen sent out by the Second Army. There was a great potential defensive line in the Semois river, a tributary of the Meuse. It was not large or deep but its steep and heavily wooded banks offered excellent opportunities to delay the invader. Failing to make contact with the Second Army's screen and fearing being outflanked, the cavalry withdrew on the 12th behind the Meuse, after blowing the bridges on the Semois. Little had been accomplished in the way of delaying the German advance, which was still on schedule.

Huntzinger had become convinced that there was a threat developing to his army but he got the axis of the attack wrong. Subsidiary and diversionary attacks by German infantry on the French town of Longwy convinced Huntzinger that the Germans were trying to turn the Maginot Line from the north and that the tank forces reported as coming through Luxembourg and southern Belgium were coming in support of this attack. The heavy fighting at Etalle added to this impression. In other words, he decided that the axis of attack of Guderian's Panzer forces was south not west. And the flank protection force at Etalle he misinterpreted as a major thrust. This ensured that he held the eastern end of his front – that is the one closest to the

11–12 May: The Passage Through the Ardennes

Maginot Line and Longwy – with his best troops and left his weakest units in defence of Sedan at the western end of his line. As a consequence, when Guderian's Panzers struck, they encountered the two B class divisions – the 55th and 71st – in the Sedan sector. One of Huntzinger's better units – a North African regular division – was moved eastwards from Sedan. He also secured reinforcements from the general reserve to be sent to defend the area around Longwy. These comprised the 3rd Armoured Division, a motorised division and a crack infantry division under Lattre de Tassigny. If not quite in the right place, they were to be more usefully placed than the other armoured divisions behind the main Belgian front.

Guderian's forces faced no great struggle for the line of the Semois river and his forces seized the key town of Bouillon on that river, although the French had successfully destroyed the bridge. On Sunday the 12th they nearly succeeded in destroying far more. Guderian had established himself in one of the best hotels in the town, which would serve as a temporary Command HQ. It was only 11 miles from Sedan. Allied aircraft had begun to visit the Ardennes sector and as Guderian began a conference with his chief of staff, a French bomb struck a German ammunition truck outside the hotel. The windows were blown in and slivers of glass flew past the Panzer commander. A large stuffed boar's head was blown off the wall and missed him by inches. Luck was once again with the Germans.

Throughout this Whit Sunday, the 1st Panzer Division advanced the last few miles to the Meuse. The bridge at Bouillon was rapidly repaired by engineers and by late in the day both the 1st and 2nd Panzer Divisions had reached the east bank of the Meuse near Sedan. It had taken fifty-seven hours. The 10th Division was still largely strung out along winding, heavily forested roads. To the north Rommel's Division also reached Dinant on the Meuse on the afternoon of the 12th. Four tanks were ordered to rush the bridge and one got within 10 yards before seeing it blown at 4.20pm. They came even closer to success a few kilometres to the north at Yvoir. The Germans actually got armoured cars onto the bridge but were frustrated by the heroism of Lieutenant De Wispelaere, of the Belgian Army, who first manned an anti-tank gun to disable the leading car and then blew the bridge. He died in the explosion. Late in the day men of Rommel's Division had a stroke of luck when a patrol discovered an undefended lock at Houx, halfway between Dinant and Yvoir. It was to have ominous consequences for the French the next day.

13–15 May: The Fall of the Netherlands

The defences of Fortress Holland were holding on the eastern side. In the north, at the eastern end of the great dike separating the IJsselmeer (Zuider Zee) from the North Sea, successful attack was almost impossible on such a narrow front. South of the IJsselmeer the Dutch forces had been pushed back to the outskirts of Utrecht but still held firm. The most ominous threat was the German presence in the southern part of Rotterdam and their bridgehead on the northern end of the Willems Bridge. However, they were still massively outnumbered by the Dutch. Welcome relief was brought when the 9th Panzer reached the Moerdijk Bridge over the Holland Deep late on the 12th, and on the 13th began to move across it and on to the south of Rotterdam over the seized bridges at Dordrecht. On the 14th von Hubicki, Commander of the Austrian Panzer Division, was shaking hands with a much-relieved – literally and metaphorically – General Kurt Student of the airborne troops.

On the 14th the Germans were preparing for a lunge north, to reinforce the bridgehead and ultimately push for Amsterdam. Encouraged by civilian authorities caught in the crossfire, there was already talk of a ceasefire and the Germans threatened the Dutch Rotterdam Commander, Colonel P. Scharroo, with an air raid on the area round the northern end of the German bridgehead if he did not surrender the city. Scharroo was told to play for time and seek confirmation of the authority of the German offer. As a result of this and a mix-up over the timing of the surrender (the Germans and Dutch were on different time systems) a raid took place on Central Rotterdam, which the Germans on the ground tried to avert but to no avail. Some of the attacking bombers did receive the order to cancel and turned away but the majority did not and dropped 97 tons of bombs on the city centre. The devastation was enormous. Over 900 were killed and 78,000 rendered homeless. Massive fires started. This was not intentional as was later believed. The Germans used high explosive not incendiaries, and the purpose was to clear a way for the attackers, not intimidate the civilians. Nevertheless, a margarine factory caught fire and produced a horrendous urban blaze with which the Dutch fire service was unable to cope. Colonel Scharroo immediately surrendered the city. The effect was to cause General Winkelman to sign a general surrender the following day for fear of devastation to other Dutch cities. Many Dutch units were outraged and wished to fight on. Others, with the Royal family and much of the Navy, left to continue the war from Britain. The short, sharp conflict caused the death of nearly 5,000 civilians and Dutch service personnel. The Germans achieved their victory at limited human cost to themselves but at the cost of enormous damage to their transport fleet of Ju 52s.

13–15 May: Battles in Central Belgium

On the 13th the battle resumed between the forces of General Höpner's XVI Army Corps and the two light mechanised divisions of General Prioux's Cavalry Corps. Höpner's forces formed the spearhead of the Sixth Army – in fact of the whole of Army Group B. It enjoyed massive superiority in tanks and could call on the support of various infantry divisions coming up behind the two Panzer divisions. It could also call on the services of VIII Corps of the Luftwaffe with 300 dive-bombers, protected by considerable numbers of fighters. The Germans, in other words, enjoyed considerable air superiority. Höpner had been ordered by VI Army HQ to break through to Gembloux and then pursue the enemy beyond. Prioux's aim was to gain time for the advancing French First Army to take up defensive positions, covering the Gembloux Gap. This meant buying time until at least the 14th.

The German attack was delayed until late in the morning, partly to await support from the Luftwaffe, which could not put in an appearance before 11am. The French fought stubbornly all afternoon losing many tanks, particularly the lightly armoured Hotchkiss tanks. Captain von Jüngenfeld described the attack as 'devilishly difficult' and was impressed with the heroic bravery of French resistance, in particular of two French artillery spotters atop a water tower on high ground. Despite certain death they continued to fire their light automatic rifles at the oncoming tanks and when finally overcome were found to have corpses like sieves, so full of holes. The two French DLMs began to pull back about 5pm. But the two German

Dunkirk and the Fall of France

Panzer divisions had not broken through. The attack was resumed earlier the next day, Tuesday 14th, and although Prioux had fulfilled his task he still did not withdraw behind the newly arrived infantry of Blanchard's Army but contested the German advance. Even at 3pm the 3rd DLM still held a position 8 kilometres in front of the First Army. The War Diary of the 3rd Panzer Division recorded later that day:

> The fact that the action of our armour-piercing weapons other than the 75mm gun has little effect on the heavy armour of the French tanks, makes the situation look critical.

In the evening Prioux finally withdrew his two divisions behind the infantry, his mission accomplished. He had tied down and slowed down superior forces enjoying air superiority. He had deliberately dispersed his forces to weaken the impact of air power and French camouflage had been excellent. Strongpoints had been bitterly contested and French tanks had often manoeuvred onto the flanks and rear of the oncoming Panzers, forcing the German tanks to return to protect their riflemen. The 3rd DLM had borne the brunt of the fighting and paid a high price, losing two-thirds of its 150 Hotchkiss tanks and one-third of its SOMUAs. The 4th Panzer Division appears to have lost 160 tanks destroyed and disabled between the 10th and 14th but since the Germans were left in possession of the battlefield, many could be repaired. The losses to the 3rd Panzer Division were smaller but even this unit had suffered moments of panic. French command and control was clearly inferior in view of the shortages of radios. One tank platoon commander records having to get out of his vehicle and tap on the turrets of his subordinates – not the most efficient way of conducting armoured warfare. One German referred to French tank gunnery as 'astoundingly bad' – a clear product of the one-man turret system. Despite these defects the quality of the French tanks in other respects, and the bravery of Prioux's troops, enabled the French Cavalry Corps to administer a hard blow to the oncoming Panzers. On Wednesday the 15th it would be the turn of the French infantry.

By the time the Cavalry Corps withdrew the infantry had effectively dug in and prepared to fight the 'methodical defensive battle' they had trained for. The French First Army was composed of first-class, highly motivated troops. The unit that was to bear the brunt of the German attack around Gembloux was the Moroccan Division, mainly composed of Moroccan regulars with an admixture of European reservists. It was commanded by a French General, Albert Mellier, who was fluent in Arabic. On either side of the Moroccans were motorised infantry divisions. The Moroccan divisional artillery had arrived on the night of 12th/13th and had had a full day to dig in and develop appropriate fire plans. The division held a 5-kilometre front around the village of Ernage, north-west of Gembloux. In artillery the French were superior to the Germans but very much inferior in the air. The first clashes had come on the afternoon of the 14th as the 3rd Panzer Division ran into the outlying Moroccan positions but were beaten off with a heavy defensive artillery barrage. Höpner decided just before 9pm to call off the attacks till the next day. He would attack at 8am with both Panzer divisions on a 6-kilometre front.

The 15th, a Wednesday, was another hot clear day. The Germans were enjoying perfect weather. Stuka attacks began on the French artillery positions at 7.30 but seem to have had minimal effect. The main attack went forward at eight o'clock as planned, led by riflemen of the 4th Panzer Division. They reached the railway line running along the front without mishap, but at 8.20 the French artillery opened up. Heavy losses were reported among both of the Panzer regiments of the 4th Division and by eleven o'clock the advance had stopped. Colonel Breith, in command of the tanks, had begun the day in the best Panzer commander fashion, nonchalantly smoking a cigar while using his radio handset in the turret of his tank. He now tried to rally the riflemen to move them forward but his vehicle was knocked out as was another coming to his rescue. He had to spend over three hours in a shell-hole and contact was lost between the divisional command and its tanks. At 15.40, Breith made it back to HQ and claimed that the artillery fire was worse than anything he had seen in the First World War and that to renew the attack on the 16th would be suicide. The Stukas tried to take out some of the Moroccans' artillery and two batteries had their guns overturned but returned to action later. Some batteries were silenced. Effective flanking fire from the artillery of the two neighbouring motorised divisions aided the Moroccan defence and these were somewhat neglected by the German dive-bombers. The 3rd Panzer Division suffered less but its assault also ground to a halt and many pulled back to their starting position. In the words of the latest historian of the Battle of Gembloux, Jeffrey Gunsburg:

> In summation at the end of a hard day of battle First Army had checked the Panzers. At no point had the enemy reached French artillery positions: the backbone of the defence was intact.

Certainly the cost to the Moroccan infantry had been severe, losing some 2,000 men, 27 per cent of the total. One of the front-line battalions had lost nearly 90 per cent. The Moroccan Division had fought with incredible bravery and although initially disconcerted by the repeated Stuka attacks had learned to disperse and not to panic. The 3rd Panzer Division had lost a quarter of its tanks since 10 May but 4th Panzer had lost nearly half and the 1st Battalion of its 12th Rifle Regiment was reduced to four officers and thirty-one men out of 700. Gunsburg concludes:

> Did the Allied *corps de bataille* of May 1940 have the weapons, the doctrine, and the motivation to confront the Blitzkrieg? The Battle of Gembloux demonstrated that the answer is yes. Here the French artillery-infantry team imposed itself handily on the German tank-plane team, despite the fact that the defence was much more improvised on open terrain than French doctrine intended, and that the German side enjoyed overwhelming air superiority.

To the north-west, German infantry assaulted the French and British along the Dyle Defence Line. The 2nd North African Division administered a bloody nose to the attacking German infantry. A French artilleryman, Pierre Porthault, of the 2nd DINA recalled his amazement and wrote an account which to many might seem like a classic description of an attack in the 1914–1918 war:

> Marching over the bodies of its brothers, which already carpeted the ground, the German infantry advanced through a hurricane of fire.

13–15 May: Crossing the Meuse and Breakout

He refers to the German action as 'uselessly superhuman'. In fact the Germans succeeded in creating a bridgehead across the Dyle at Limal but pulled back on the 16th.

To their north, the British 2nd Division faced attacks and Second Lieutenant Dick Annand of the Durham Light Infantry won the VC for driving back a party of German infantry who were attempting to establish a bridgehead near the village of Gastuche. Annand attacked groups of German infantry three times with hand grenades, later claiming that he was so confused by the firing that he believed himself to be dead. The British launched such a powerful artillery bombardment accompanying a limited counter-attack towards the end of the day that panic was induced in the German 31st Infantry Division. To the west the 3rd British Division under Montgomery defended Louvain from German attacks. As always, Montgomery tended to retire early, confident that he had everything under control and he could trust his subordinates. He was irritated to be woken by a staff officer, telling him that the Germans had got into Louvain on the night of 14/15th. He was told in no uncertain terms: 'Go away and don't bother me. Tell the Brigadier in Louvain to throw them out.' His diary records:

> Enemy attacked on Left of the Royal Ulster Rifles and got into Louvain Station. Counter-attacked and pushed out (10.00hrs). At 13.30hrs attack developed on Coldstream front; heavy shelling all afternoon; Coldstream suffered severe casualties but front intact.

The British line, like the French, was holding. Unfortunately, events further east and south along the Meuse were not going so well and it was developments there that led both the British and the French First Army to decide to withdraw from the Dyle Line that they had reached and defended in good order.

13–15 May: Crossing the Meuse and Breakout

During these three days, on a 50-mile stretch of the Meuse valley, the fate of France and Europe was to be decided. There was nothing certain about the outcome. The German attackers had numerous advantages but so, too, did the defenders. The Germans had achieved surprise, thrusting through an unexpected area in record time. They enjoyed air supremacy. They also struck against two of the weaker French Armies with a greater proportion of elderly (30+) reservists who were also under-equipped. Corap's Ninth Army of seven divisions held 70 miles of front. The textbooks recommended 6 miles per division. Two divisions had no anti-tank guns and there was a serious shortage of anti-aircraft guns. The northern section of Corap's Army had had to march 75 miles from the Belgian border to take up their positions around Dinant and relieve the Belgian Chasseurs, thinly holding the line of the River Meuse. Many only arrived on the 13th to find themselves facing an attack that was already under way. Three Panzer corps formed the steel tips of Rundstedt's Army Group A. In the north, the XV under Hoth, comprising the 5th and 7th Panzers had reached the Meuse on Whit Sunday, the 12th, but found, as described above, all the bridges blown. They were nevertheless the first into action and the first to get men across. Reinhardt's XLI, comprising the 6th and 5th Panzers, had the slowest journey to the Meuse, reaching Montherme with a few advanced units late on the 12th. In the south, facing the western end of Huntzinger's 2nd Army at Sedan, was the strongest of the steel tips under Guderian and composed of three Panzer divisions, the 1st, 2nd and 10th. The fact that both Reinhardt's and Guderian's forces – five Panzer divisions in all – were striking the junction of two under-equipped French armies was another considerable advantage to the attacker. The weather was also excellent.

Nevertheless, the French position was by no means hopeless. The line of the Meuse presented a formidable defensive obstacle to the Germans, very different from the flat plain around Gembloux. The River Meuse was far more formidable as a barrier than the Dyle. It was on average 60 metres wide and fairly fast flowing and unfordable. On the western banks were steep wooded slopes, ideal for defence. Just to the north of Houx, where Rommel's men had found a lightly guarded weir, were the heights of Wastia, which commanded the whole line of the river to the south. They were a terrifying prospect to seize. One German soldier described the Meuse's western bank as being guarded by 'fire-spitting mountains'. Reinhardt's point of arrival on the Meuse was even worse with 1,000-foot rocky heights towering over the little town of Montherme, and here the 42nd Colonial Machine Gun Brigade had time to dig in. At Sedan, again, the west bank rose steeply and the French had constructed concrete bunkers about every 500m, some 200–300 metres from the bank. These were linked and strengthened in places by barbed wire and field defences. Crossing the Meuse and gaining the high ground before making a breakout would be no push-over. The bulk of Rundstedt's forces were still trailing slowly on foot with horse and carts through the Ardennes. No wonder Halder, the Chief of Staff, had given the plan only a one-in-ten chance of success.

The Northern Spearpoint

Clearly the intact sluice at Houx, halfway between Yvoir and Dinant, was a weak spot and here the Germans had yet another stroke of the very generous dollops of luck that were handed out to them during this campaign. A French engineering colonel in the 5th Division of Corap's Army had already noticed the weak spot and told a young lieutenant to pass the warning to his infantry colonel so that the spot could be held more strongly. The infantry colonel was in fact killed at Dinant on the afternoon of the 12th and the warning never passed on. Rommel's motorcycle battalion, which discovered the sluice, was able to cross during the hours of darkness and early morning mist, and establish themselves up the slopes on the other side of the river. They were lightly armed, and their hold on the western slope precarious, but it was the first pebble to fall in what became an avalanche, destroying the French position. As light came the crossing became more dangerous. More French troops were coming up and the fire on the crossing increased. Several were killed and wounded but the battalion commander gradually got most of his men across and began to push on to the high ground, taking the small settlement of La Grange. But they were armed with nothing more than light machine guns and tenuously linked to the eastern bank.

South of Houx, Rommel's Division had been attempting another crossing at the village of Bouvignes since dawn, using rubber assault boats. Here the action was by the 6th Rifle Regiment under Colonel von Bismarck. He had managed to get a company across the river but the fire was increasing and boats and men were being shot to pieces. When Rommel arrived at the scene the crossing was stalled. He ordered some neighbouring houses to be set on fire, in the hope that the smoke would cover the crossing, and brought tanks down to the river edge to provide counter-battery work against the bunkers on the French side. Despite continuing heavy casualties more began to make it across and a cable ferry using pontoons began to be constructed. Rommel appears to have provided frenzied leadership. He crossed the Meuse to see the position for himself and urged the riflemen up a deep gully to the higher ground. Returning to the east bank, Rommel then went north in a tank to Houx, where things were improving and the engineers were building pontoon bridges to float vehicles across. However, by the morning of the 14th, only fifteen tanks were on the western bank and Rommel's forces were still lodged precariously with pockets of French defenders still inside the small German bridgehead. What is amazing is the sloth of the French commanders in responding on the 13th. Counter-attacks were repeatedly postponed. The day ended with a brief attack of unsupported tanks, which captured a few German prisoners, but lacking infantry support then withdrew. The day was one of the turning points of the campaign. In the words of Alistair Horne, in his classic account, *To Lose a Battle*:

> A golden opportunity to wipe out Rommel's bridgehead and inflict a serious reverse upon him had been lost. All that day events had been balanced on a knife edge – much more finely balanced, indeed than was apparent to the French defenders at the time. Without Rommel's personal leadership on the one side, with just a little more determination on the other, the story might have been different.

The events of the 14th were determined by the same three forces: Rommel's energy and aggression, French sloth and caution, and luck. Despite French threats to his tenuous hold on Wastia, the crucial high ground to the north of Houx, Rommel struck out with a small force of thirty tanks on the main road from Dinant aiming to gain control of the flat, rolling, high ground around the town of Onhaye – the perfect assembly point for tank breakout to the west. Rommel himself was nearly killed and his tank wrecked, sliding down a steep slope to finish on its side. His signal's command vehicle was also hit and he himself nearly captured by the excellent North African infantry of the division moved up to contain the threat.

The Northern Spearpoint

These troops were part of the best division in the Ninth Army, and if used decisively that day, could still have turned the scales. They were used to contain the German attack rather than push it back. If it had been used with the 1st Armoured Division, coming up from the west, then 7th Panzer would have been in trouble; but the French Tank Division was late assembling and lacked fuel. Rommel's push west had a terrifying effect on the Ninth Army. There were signs of panic and crumbling morale. Stories circulated of German breakthroughs and German tanks to the rear of infantry positions. The Stukas ranged unchecked overhead. To the south of Rommel and his growing force at Onhaye, the French 22nd Division began to crack without really facing a major attack. The divisional chief of staff, in the absence of the divisional commander, ordered a retreat from the Meuse. The corps commander ordered the 18th (opposite Houx) back as well. A vast hole had been opened for the Germans to exploit on the 15th.

General André-Georges Corap, the commander of the battered Ninth Army, was no fool. He was sixty-two and becoming slightly corpulent but he was popular with his troops, with a reputation for caring for their welfare. He had been top of his class many years before, when he passed out as an officer cadet at St Cyr, and had performed well both during the First World War and in North Africa during the 1920s. Since being appointed to his command he had repeatedly stressed the lack of crucial equipment but had been fobbed off with assurances of the tranquillity of his sector. Now that the sector was anything but tranquil he had to make a critical decision. At two o'clock in the early hours of Wednesday the 15th, he telephoned his immediate superior with the news that he intended to withdraw from the line of the Meuse to the original line on the frontier, from which his army had laboriously advanced on the 10th. The advance of Rommel against the 18th Division, the breaking up of the 22nd and the threat to his southern flank around Sedan (see below) convinced him that the methodical battle and the continuous front necessitated withdrawal. He totally underestimated the speed of mobile warfare and the shattering effect such an attempted move would have. His superior, General Billotte, agreed but insisted on an intermediate halt line along the Charleroi–Rethel road. Ironically, it ran through Rocroi, where 300 years before the French had defeated the Spanish and made themselves the greatest power in Europe. No such victory was to come now, in 1940. Corap's decision unleashed the avalanche that had been building for two days. The critical position of the early morning became a rout.

Rommel was done with consolidation around Onhaye and proposed to break out west. He aimed to reach 8 miles beyond Billotte's halt line in one day. At 8am he received the welcome news that dive-bomber support would be available from the Luftwaffe. The other Panzer Division of Hoth's Corps was coming up behind Rommel and provided some protection to his flank. Almost directly in front of Rommel's line of advance was the French 1st Armoured Division, re-routed from the Gembloux Gap to support Corap's front. Its commander, General Bruneau, had made the mistake of placing the refuelling trucks at the very rear of the division and the chaos of the roads with their floods of pitiable refugees slowed their advance. Many of the division's 170 tanks were in need of refuelling. First, Bruneau's halted tanks near the village of Flavion were caught by Stukas and then, at about 8.30, by Rommel's advancing Panzers. As usual he charged straight in, spraying bullets and shells at the surprised Frenchmen. The Char Bs seemed impervious to German shells and the damage they might have inflicted, if used effectively and if ready for action, can only be guessed at. Many French tanks simply had to be abandoned and the Germans were able to move freely round their opponents, often finding some vulnerable spot, which the heavy armour did not protect. As the 5th Panzer Division came up, Rommel broke off the action with the 7th and rushed on to the west, leaving the 5th to clean up. At times particular groups of French tanks were able to use their superior armour and punch to knock out German tanks and perhaps 100 in all were damaged and destroyed, but by the end of the day Bruneau's Division was left with twenty out of its original 170. One of the strongest assets in the French Army had ceased to exist.

Rommel pushed on, into the rear areas of the Ninth Army, causing mayhem. He reached Philippeville by noon. At various points he encountered groups of surprised French soldiers. He overtook artillery sent to the rear by the 4th North African Division, which had given him a hard time the previous day, and added to the terror and confusion that now infected the whole of Corap's Army. Dive-bombed and prey to rumours of German tanks behind and in front, the 18th and 22nd Divisions seem to have disintegrated. Deprived of its artillery the 4th North African was cut to pieces as it tried to withdraw. Rommel finally halted his tired and triumphant troops well behind the halt line envisaged by the French High Command. Corap's order to withdraw had engendered disaster.

Reinhardt's Spearpoint

The experience of the central spearpoint was very different from that of Hoth's Corps, which had had the easiest passage to the Meuse. A slow journey through the most difficult terrain of the Ardennes was marred by traffic jams and conflict with Guderian's 2nd Panzer Division, which had strayed onto the wrong road. When at last the leading members of Reinhardt's Corps reached the Meuse at Montherme, late on the 12th, it was to find first-class French troops well dug in. The Germans' opponents were regulars of the 102nd Fortress Division. They were short of artillery but made up for it with courage and determination. For two days the machine-gunners from Madagascar and French Indo China held up the riflemen of the 6th Panzer Division. For them the order to withdraw on the 15th was a double disaster – as a fortress division they had no transport. On the 15th they were overwhelmed and as the Panzers now broke out they rounded up the gallant defenders of the Montherme crossing. To their north another B Division of the Ninth disintegrated as it tried to retreat. Reinhardt's tanks raced westwards, causing even more panic and astonishment than Rommel to the north. The industrial city of Charleville-Mézières fell. French units surrendered without a fight. Confusion and panic undermined any effective resistance. The most tragic loss was the destruction of the French 2nd Armoured Division or DCR. Its fate was more ignominious than that of the 1st at Flavion. It had been held in reserve at Chalons and was ordered first to Charleroi, to join in the attack on Rommel, then diverted further south. Tanks were sent on trains separate from the rest of the division's transport and artillery. Consequently, it was caught piecemeal by the advancing 6th and 8th Panzers and simply brushed aside without achieving anything. By the end of the day the Panzer Corps was at Montcornet on the River Serre, 40 miles west of Sedan.

Dunkirk and the Fall of France

The Crossing of the Meuse at Sedan and Breakout

If Rocroi was the scene of a famous French victory, Sedan was pregnant with historical gloom for France. It was the place where the Prussians had inflicted defeat in 1870, ending the period of French European dominance begun at Rocroi. Now all depended on the 55th Division on the extreme left of Huntzinger's Second Army. It was a B Division of somewhat elderly reservists. The average age of the ordinary soldiers was thirty-one, the average captain forty-two. It was exceptionally well supplied with artillery, like much of the French Army, but had only fifty-six anti-tank guns to cover its 17-kilometre front. To try to shorten its frontage the 71st Division was ordered up from training to take over a section just east of Sedan, releasing two of the 55th's battalions to strengthen the key section opposite the city itself. The 71st had arrived just in time but the two released battalions did not take up their new positions before the attack began. Anti-tank mines and anti-aircraft guns were also in short supply. Despite this its position was a strong one. Bunkers had been built at 500-yard intervals and although most of Sedan on the eastern shore of the river was indefensible, the river and bunkers on the western shore presented a formidable obstacle. Behind the bunkers the ground rose steeply to the forested Marfee Heights, which commanded excellent views of the German attackers and excellent emplacements for the batteries of artillery. The German Panzers were particularly vulnerable as they crowded into every conceivable space on the east bank of the Meuse. Luckily for them, the French Corps Commander, General Grandsard, limited firing to thirty shells per gun, believing the battle would be a long one, and that a serious German attack could not start for five or six days, until more of the German artillery had come up.

In fact, the Germans were short of heavy guns and ammunition. What there were had only fifty rounds each, the ammunition lorries being stuck in the seemingly endless traffic jams on the winding roads of the Ardennes. The position was so bad that even Hurrying Heinz Guderian wished to delay the attack for another day, to give time for greater artillery support and for his tired men to rest. He was overruled by his normally cautious superior, von Kleist, who determined that the attack should go in on the afternoon of the 13th. It is only possible to speculate what would have been the effect of a

The Crossing of the Meuse at Sedan and Breakout

day's delay and an unrestrained bombardment of the crowded, waiting Germans. There was no shortage of ammunition on the French side and four days later most of it was in German hands. Kleist's decision in this case proved correct and detrimental to the French chances of holding the line of the Meuse.

But a second decision by von Kleist was mistaken, according to Guderian. The two generals appreciated the vital importance of aircraft in silencing – or at least weakening – the French artillery. Seven hundred and ten German aircraft were available to facilitate the crossing but von Kleist and Guderian disagreed as to how they should be used. Guderian had agreed with Lorzer, the Luftwaffe commander, that a pattern of sustained bombing by repeated waves of approximately forty aircraft was best. Von Kleist favoured a massive concentrated air bombardment prior to the crossing and overruled Guderian. Luckily his order arrived too late and Guderian got the type of air support he had requested and felt was essential for success. Once again the fates were with the German attackers. The cloudless sky was another bonus.

The impact of the air attacks was almost everything that Guderian had hoped for. The casualties were not great but the disruption of the defenders was. Controlling telephone cables were cut, leaving batteries and blockhouses isolated. Fighters machine-gunned any man who moved and most importantly, the noise and tension sapped the will to resist. A young French intelligence officer on the Marfee Heights described the horror: 'The Stukas join the heavy bombers. The siren of the dive-bombers bores into one's ears and puts one's nerves on edge. They make you want to scream.' He described his cipher clerk repeating over and over again: 'This one's going to land on us. This is it ...'

Despite the ferocity of the air assault, crossing the Meuse was no picnic and at times came close to failure. The 2nd Panzer Division, on the extreme right of the German attack, encountered particular difficulties. It arrived at the river late on the 13th after a slow slog through the hills of the Ardennes and endless traffic jams. Two crossings were attempted on both sides of the village of Donchery, 2 miles from Sedan. A few troops made it across but the resistance from the French bunkers was fierce and those not killed or wounded had to swim back. The division's tanks tried to knock out the bunkers firing across the river but failed. Only after the bunkers were attacked from the rear by elements of the more successful 1st Division did the 2nd secure any sort of lodgement on the south side at about 10pm. The 10th Panzer Division's attack on the left was nearly as sterile. Large numbers of boats were shot up by French artillery and machine-gun fire and the attack appeared to falter, but under cover of smoke and dust two small groups made it to the southern side in the few remaining boats. Everything turned on individual heroism. One such hero was Lieutenant Hanbauer, who crossed at Wadelincourt and knocked out key bunkers and then advanced rapidly to capture the heights overlooking the crossing. Another group of assault engineers, under Sergeant Rubarth, showed amazing courage and enjoyed considerable luck, knocking out bunker after bunker and clearing the way for two infantry battalions of the division to cross late on the 13th. A propaganda account published in 1942 recalls the heroics:

> Death stares across from the bunkers on the other side of the river. The machine guns are shaving the flat terrain. The Meuse is 80 metres wide at this point – that means covering 80 metres while offering target practice for the enemy. The two rubber boats are prepared; they only carry three men each, but one will have to take four; Rubarth, Corporal Theophel, and Lance-Corporals Brautigam and Podszus. The other seven members of the platoon will follow at a distance. The boats are launched into the water, and the men fall rather than climb into the narrow rubber dinghy. The boat starts to spin and the four assault pioneers aren't moving until Rubarth takes the rudder himself. 'Shoot, Podszus!' he roars into his comrade's ear; it is important above all to hold down the fire from the bunker nearest to the bank.
>
> One jump and they are on the bank, without loss. Rubarth makes for the first bunker. Podszus jumps up on top of the bunker. Rubarth hurls his explosive charge into the embrasure – Podszus lurks above the reinforced door, hand grenades at the ready. There is an explosion that makes your ears ring. The occupants open the door, Podszus throws in a hand-grenade – they all come out with their hands up.

The Crossing of the Meuse at Sedan and Breakout

However, despite all Rubarth's and Hanbauer's heroism, the day ended with the 10th Division clinging precariously to a small bridgehead with the French still in a strong position on the high ground around Noyers.

It was the success of the central attack by the 1st Division that decided the issue. Here the hero was a slightly more senior officer, Lieutenant-Colonel Hermann Balck. He was one of the most outstanding leaders of fighting men in the German or any other army. He was commander of the First Infantry Regiment of the 1st Panzer Division. The regiment was the equivalent to a British brigade. Balck's ancestors had served in the British Army, his great-grandfather being a member of Wellington's Staff in the Peninsula. Two of Balck's battalions crossed the Meuse at 3pm, close to an abandoned cloth factory in the Sedan suburb of Gaulier. Subdued by the air attacks, the French defenders were rolled up and bunker after bunker captured. The advancing Germans soon reached the Château of Bellevue, where the French had surrendered in 1870. They pressed on to higher ground, achieving a penetration of $3^1/_2$ miles by 10pm and dug in around the small town of Cheveuges. Their advance made possible a successful crossing by the 2nd Panzer Division late in the day, as Balck's men had turned the flank of the defenders at Donchery. Another more difficult crossing was achieved by the Gross Deutschland Regiment, attached to 1st Panzer. This was half a mile east of Balck's crossing but fierce fighting limited the degree of penetration on the 13th. For the French, the most ominous development of the day was the rapid construction of rafts and a pontoon bridge to facilitate transport across the river. Two rafts were ferrying heavier equipment across before 8pm. This included anti-aircraft guns. By 11pm a pontoon bridge was operational and the tanks could begin to cross. Clearly a massive counterstroke was necessary on the 14th to prevent disaster for France and the whole Allied cause.

The commander of the French 55th Division had two infantry regiments and two battalions of light tanks available for a counter-attack on Balck by 7pm on the 13th. He did nothing with them till the morning of the 14th. It was a disastrous delay. The attack went in early in the morning of the 14th and met with initial success against the lightly equipped German infantry, but soon Panzers rapidly pushed across the pontoon bridge, turned the tide, and crushed the light French tanks. Psychologically, this was a shattering blow for the whole 55th Division, already badly mauled the previous day. Panic began to spread and wild rumours circulated of massive breakthroughs of German tanks. The 55th was no longer an effective fighting force: some surrendered; many more retreated. The panic spread to the largely unused 71st Division, also composed of elderly reservists. The cry of 'Tanks!' passed from one section to another. Riflemen, machine-gunners and artillerymen all fled. It was said that by 2pm on the 14th no one was left in position. Grandsard's Corps, defending the front at Sedan, had ceased to exist. With the disintegration of the 55th Division, 10th Panzer seized the heights around Noyers in the early afternoon.

The Allied Air Forces, however, did demonstrate gallantry on the 14th, but it was heroic futility. Recognising the importance of the Meuse bridges, both the French Armée de L'Air and the air component of the British Field Force were thrown into the assault. Some 152 bombers and 250 fighters took part. The British light bombers, Fairey Battles, were massacred by both German fighters and in particular by the effective flak batteries put together by Guderian's Corps around the crossing points. Oberst (Colonel) von Hippel, watching the scene, recalled:

> We could not help admiring the guts displayed by our opponents in attacking the bridges again and again despite all their losses and the fierce flak fire, and even shooting from planes already on fire, wounding some of our artillerymen.

Of seventy-one British bombers taking part, forty were shot down, plus a further thirty-one fighters. Another watching German officer recorded the scene:

> Again and again an enemy aircraft crashes out of the sky, dragging a long plume of smoke behind it, which after the crash of the succeeding explosion remains for some time perpendicular in the warm air. Occasionally from the falling machines one or two white parachutes release themselves and float slowly to earth. In the short time that I am at the bridge, barely an hour, eleven planes were brought down.

The Crossing of the Meuse at Sedan and Breakout

The official RAF history records that 'No higher rate of loss has ever been experienced by the Royal Air Force.' No significant damage was inflicted on the Meuse crossing points. Tanks and equipment continued to flood across into the expanding bridgehead.

Guderian and his superiors now had to take crucial decisions. Caution would indicate consolidation of the bridgehead. In particular there was a growing threat to the south of the German position as the French deployed the 3rd Armoured Division and the 3rd Motorised Division, under General Flavigny, near to the ridge of high ground around the village of Stonne. This would threaten the German flank. Flavigny wished to attack early on the 14th but the commander of the 3rd Armoured, General Brocard, insisted on a delay till the 15th. The division had only been formed in March and was under-prepared for action. Eventually, Flavigny changed his mind about an attack on the 14th and the tanks were dug in to help plug a defensive 12-mile line. Thus another French opportunity was wasted.

Guderian made no such error, and at a hastily convened conference with the Staff of the 1st Panzer Division, decided to go for broke. It was to be one of the most crucial decisions of the campaign. Recognising the signs of disintegration in the French Army, he swung the 1st and 2nd Panzers westwards with orders to advance towards Rethel on the Aisne, 40 kilometres from Sedan. One of the Staff officers answered Guderian's invitation for advice with one of Hurrying Heinz's own favourite expressions: 'Boot them, don't tap them!' ('Klotzen, nicht Kleckern!') Boot them he certainly intended to do. To hold the flank against Flavigny he detached the 10th Panzer and the Gross Deutschland Regiment. Their orders were to thrust towards Stonne, 20 kilometres south of Sedan, and thus to hold open the breach in the French front until relieved by the slowly advancing 16th and 24th Infantry Divisions. It was a bold strategic decision and the subsequent outcome marked Guderian as a soldier of genius. A decisive French thrust into the lightly guarded German flank could have turned German triumph into defeat. The 1st Panzer Division itself was suffering from fuel and ammunition shortages and only a quarter of the tanks were combat-ready as it launched itself west.

The 10th Division had not fully deployed across the Meuse and the initial defence of the flank would depend on the already exhausted

Gross Deutschland Regiment. Guderian was certainly taking a gamble. The fighting that developed around the hilltop village of Stonne on the 15th was to become the most bitter and prolonged of the Battle of the Sedan bridgehead. Despite their weakness and fatigue, Gross Deutschland did not sit on the defensive but attacked the high ground around Stonne at 7am on the 15th. This triggered a French counter-attack, which somewhat disrupted the systematic battle planned by Flavigny, scheduled to begin at 3pm. The French had hoped to drive north in three clear phases in the best 1918 tradition and thereby regain the Marfee Heights above the crossings at Sedan. By 11am the French had regained Stonne and pushed back the worn out Gross Deutschland Regiment. In the afternoon, infantry from 10th Panzer helped recapture the village, but just after 5pm they were forced out again. Clearly the Germans were under serious pressure. The heavy French Char Bs appeared formidable and as one German account records:

> The fire of the three heavy tanks threatens to wipe out the anti-tank section. But it remains in position. One moment one of the colossuses crosses the front. The left gun commander, Corporal Giesemann, discovers in the middle of its right side a small-ribbed surface; apparently it is the radiator! It is not much bigger than an ammunition box. He aims at it. A tongue of flame shoots out of the tank.

Giesemann had discovered what other German soldiers had discovered on the same day at Flavion in their battle with the 1st DCR, the weakpoint of the Char B.

Despite this, the battle was touch-and-go and if only the French had effectively concentrated their tank forces, success might have been achieved. There was nothing wrong with the morale of the French tank crews and the Germans spoke highly of their bravery. The attack proved indecisive because of the skill of the German anti-tank companies and the fact that French forces were thrown in piecemeal. Two tank battalions of the 3rd DCR never took part in the attacks of the 15th, yet 10th Panzer and Gross Deutschland had been stretched to the limit. When Brocard called off the attacks on the evening of the 15th, perhaps the last chance of French victory had been lost.

The Crossing of the Meuse at Sedan and Breakout

The fighting around Stonne also had a disastrous effect on French strategic calculations. The ferocity of the fighting and the use of 10th Panzer temporarily convinced the French High Command that the main German thrust was south from Sedan not west. They feared an attack around the back of the Maginot Line or south-west to Paris. This misconception aided the real thrust westwards to the Channel coast.

Guderian's 1st and 2nd Division had a harder time of it in their turn to the west than either Rommel had in Belgium or Reinhardt had with his corps in his impressive dash to Montcornet. The French High Command had begun to build up a force to plug the gap, opened by the German crossing of the Meuse. It was eventually to become a new Sixth Army, under General Touchon, and it was being assembled north of the Aisne and west of the Ardennes canal. The key component of this new force was the Second DCR, and as indicated above, it was wiped out as a fighting force by Reinhardt's sudden advance. The other key unit in Touchon's force was the excellent 14th Infantry Division, under General Lattre de Tassigny. It had been withdrawn from Lorraine and was being reassembled for action as Guderian began his advance. A single French company held up the advance at Chagny with heroic resistance, and further bitter fighting took place further west at Bouvellement with other elements of Tassigny's Division, but only one regiment could be brought up in time. Just to the north, at the village of La Horgne, a North African brigade of cavalry fought ferociously till 6pm, by which time it had been effectively wiped out. On the German side, Lieutenant-Colonel Balck was once again the hero. Guderian himself recalls the events in his memoirs:

> ammunition was running low. The men in the front line were falling asleep in their slit trenches. Balck himself, in wind jacket and with a knotty stick in his hand, told me that the capture of the village had only succeeded because when his officers complained against continuation of the attack, he had replied: 'In that case I'll take the place on my own!' and had moved off. His men had thereupon followed him. His dirty face and red-rimmed eyes showed that he had spent a hard day and a sleepless night. For his doings on that day he was to receive the

Knight's Cross. His opponents – a good Norman infantry division and a brigade of Spahis – had fought bravely. The enemy's machine guns were still firing into the village street, but for some time now there had been no artillery fire and Balck shared my opinion that resistance was almost over.

Guderian was right in seeing this ferocious defence as the last throw of the French Army in its attempt to prevent breakout. By the end of the 15th a huge bulge had been created in the French line, cutting off the First Army in Belgium and the BEF from the French forces to the south. There was hardly anything facing the unleashed seven Panzer divisions should they head west. Now, for the first time, Blitzkrieg was to be put into practice to doom the Allies. As Premier Reynaud had telephoned Churchill earlier in the day: 'We have lost the battle.'

This battle for the Sedan bridgehead was the decisive battle of the campaign. It had been won primarily by the German infantry, not the tanks. It had involved extraordinary heroism on the part of individual German soldiers but also a lot of luck. Victory was not inevitable. This view is echoed by the leading expert on this crucial phase of the campaign, Robert A. Doughty:

> Among the important insights provided by this new material is the recognition of how precarious the German victory at Sedan actually was. Although the Germans concentrated three of their best Army divisions against one of the French weakest, only three of their six major crossings succeeded. Had the French managed to prevent even one of the three successful crossings – and they almost did – the scale and pace of subsequent fighting would have been decidedly different. Guderian acknowledged in his memoirs how fortunate the Germans were by characterising their success as 'almost a miracle'.

16–20 May: The Race to the Channel

John Colville, the private secretary of the new British Prime Minister, began his diary entry for Sunday the 19th with the words: 'Heavenly weather again. It has been cloudless for at least three weeks now and we can none of us really profit by it.'

16–20 May: The Race to the Channel

If a British civil servant could not profit by it, the same could not be said of the German Panzers and the Luftwaffe. As in so many other ways, the German attackers were incredibly lucky with the weather in May 1940. Their tanks could race across Northern France assisted by the free ranging German aircraft operating in cloudless skies. During these five days, Guderian's chief problem was the caution of his superiors, fearful that the Panzers were going too far too fast. Hitler, von Rundstedt and von Kleist all fretted that disaster was round the corner and triumphal breakthrough could be transformed into catastrophe by the overenthusiastic behaviour of Rommel, Reinhardt, and above all, Guderian. They were mindful of the events of September 1914, when after initial defeats and setbacks – as great as the ones inflicted on the French by 15 May 1940 – a French counter-attack had forced the Germans back and led to four years of stalemate. This would spell disaster for Nazi Germany, far less prepared for a long struggle than the Second Reich of the Kaiser. Churchill's famous phrase, describing events on the 18th, that 'the tortoise is thrusting his head very far beyond his carapace', echoed this assessment. Neither Hitler nor von Rundstedt fully appreciated the concept of Blitzkrieg as preached by Guderian and embraced by Rommel. Both of these were prepared to take enormous risks on the assumption that the French must be kept off-balance while their morale was crumbling. Speed and aggression was everything. Von Rundstedt – who also appreciated the delicate psychology of war – drew the conclusion that at all costs the French must not be allowed a victory to restore their self-confidence: hence the need to consolidate and avoid the risks some of his subordinates were intent on taking. Tensions within the German command structure over these issues were to produce blazing rows during the third week of May. They were, however, tensions arising from the vision of crushing victory.

Meanwhile, tensions increasingly showed themselves on the Allied side as a result of the looming catastrophe. General Georges and Gamelin, his nominal superior, had never liked one another and defeat did not improve their relationship. Corap was sacked from his command of the Ninth Army and replaced by Giraud, but the army had virtually ceased to exist. The most important French head to fall was that of Gamelin himself. On the 17th his predecessor, General

Dunkirk and the Fall of France

Maxim Weygand, was summoned from his command in Syria to return to Paris. The French Prime Minister had never had much faith in the fighting spirit of Gamelin, but could think of no more original choice as a replacement than the former chief of staff who had stepped down in 1935. A 73-year-old was replacing a 68-year-old. Weygand was certainly filled with fighting spirit and his small, neat frame conveyed the impression of a fighting bantam cock. Gamelin handed over without any show of reluctance on the 20th. Weygand is supposed to have tapped his briefcase on his arrival and reassured those who greeted him that the case contained the secrets of Marshal Foch's success in 1918 but, as the historian A. J. P. Taylor has pointed out, the case was empty.

Defeat also ratcheted up the tensions between the Allies. The British had little faith in the Belgians on their left flank and increasingly felt that their French allies were little better. The morale of Gort's superior, General Billotte, seemed to have collapsed like the front at Sedan. The French feared that the British might cut and run. They certainly wanted Britain to make available far more aircraft by deploying another ten squadrons of fighters to France. The seriousness of the situation was emphasised by Churchill's decision to fly to Paris on the 16th. The visit was not reassuring. The British Prime Minister and his two military advisers, Dill and Ismay, met Gamelin, Reynaud and Daladier. Churchill recalled:

> Utter dejection was written on every face. In front of Gamelin, on a student's easel, was a map about 2 yards square, with a black ink line purporting to show the Allied front. In this line there was drawn a small sinister bulge at Sedan.
>
> The Commander-in-Chief briefly explained what had happened. North and south of Sedan, on a front of 50 or 60 miles, the Germans had broken through. The French Army in front of them was destroyed or scattered. A heavy onrush of armoured vehicles was advancing with unheard-of speed towards Amiens and Arras, with the intention, apparently, of reaching the coast at Abbeville or thereabouts. Alternatively they might make for Paris. Behind the armour, he said, eight or ten German divisions, all motorised, were driving onwards, making flanks for themselves as they advanced against two

disconnected French Armies on either side. The General talked perhaps five minutes without anyone saying a word. When he stopped there was a considerable silence. I then asked: 'Where is the strategic reserve?' and, breaking into French, which I used indifferently (in every sense): 'Ou est la masse de manoeuvre?' General Gamelin turned to me, and, with a shake of his head and a shrug, said: 'Aucune.'

There was a another long pause. Outside in the garden of the Quay d'Orsay clouds of smoke arose from large bonfires, and I saw from the window venerable officials pushing wheelbarrows of archives on to them. Already therefore the evacuation of Paris was being prepared.

Churchill and the Cabinet initially agreed to the French request for ten more fighter squadrons but the bitter protests of Dowding, Head of Fighter Command, that this would totally undermine the air defence of the UK led to the decision being reversed on the 19th. No more aircraft would go to France but would operate from forward bases in southern England. To the French this looked like betrayal of the Allied cause.

The German Advance

Bitter fighting continued around Stonne on the 16th but despite the ferocity of the French artillery bombardments – terrifying to the newly arriving German infantry – this crucial shoulder of the German breakout became bogged down in stalemate. The French had thrown away their armoured reserves and the German elite formation, Gross Deutschland, was pulled out for a well-earned rest. The key point of attack now moved further west. It nearly didn't. Guderian's commander von Kleist was clearly nervous at the thought of his Panzers getting too far ahead of the infantry and ordered a halt on the evening of the 15th till the bridgehead was consolidated. Guderian was furious and after a heated argument with his superior got reluctant permission for a further 24-hour advance to make space for the advancing infantry in the bridgehead. Guderian rushed on. As he himself wrote:

The fog of war that had confused us soon lifted. We were in the open now [...] The men were wide awake and aware that we had achieved a complete victory, a breakthrough.

Dunkirk and the Fall of France

The 1st and 2nd Panzers pressed on to Montcornet, where they found the 6th of Rheinhardt's Corps. The big problem was allotting roads to avoid snarl-ups. There was now little sign of the French. One of the officers on the Staff of the 1st Panzer recalled that the chief noise was from the bellowing of unmilked cows as the civilian population had fled, leaving these increasingly discomforted animals to be relieved of their burden by the Germans. By the end of the day the leading units had covered 40 miles and were 55 miles west of Sedan.

To the north, Rommel made even more startling progress with the 7th Panzer Division. Told to advance to the French frontier from his starting point in south-east Belgium, he reached the border defences near Clairfayts early in the evening. Blockhouses and barbed wire represented a weak extension of the Maginot Line. However, once again the Germans were lucky: the covering French artillery were not stocked up with shells and failed to lay down the formidable barrage that they should have been capable of. French infantry units were shattered: first, by their advance into Belgium and then their disorderly retreat. Remnants of the heroic 4th North African Division were asked to fight after marching 70 miles without rations. Having successfully broken through, Rommel did not halt but advanced at night towards Le Cateau via the town of Avesnes. Here there was a brief fight with the remains of the 1st DCR, but for the most part Rommel encountered only chaos. Columns of refugees intermingled with French troops, too astonished by the presence of the Germans to resist. Sometimes the French appeared to believe these foreigners were 'Les Anglais'. They were rapidly disabused and told to surrender, which most did. Rommel led the advance like a junior officer, miles from his HQ and often out of radio contact. At Landrecies he found an undamaged bridge across the Sambre and drove into the town rounding up French troops in the barracks and sending them off eastwards. By 5.15 on the morning of the 17th he was nearly at Le Cateau and had advanced 55 miles. For the loss of one officer and forty men he had taken 10,000 prisoners and knocked out 100 tanks. Out of petrol and almost out of ammunition, it was a remarkable but incredibly risky achievement. A thin and brittle spear had been thrust through the remains of the Ninth Army and by crossing the Sambre, Rommel had destroyed yet another planned French line of defence. It was the triumph of bold cheek over common sense. Yet it had worked and contributed enormously to the tide of despair now drowning the senior commanders of the French Army.

But anxiety was gnawing at many of the senior German commanders from Hitler down. Only Halder, the Chief of the General Staff, had completely overcome his initial pessimism and now felt that the French were beaten. He even proposed the risky strategy of compressing the campaign into one operation, leaving von Bock to finish off the British and the French in Belgium and throwing the Panzers ahead of schedule southwards. Hitler would hear none of it and his nerves struck a chord with von Rundstedt, Commander of Army Group A. Both were desperate to avoid a replay of 1914. The young von Rundstedt's unit had actually been in sight of Paris in that year and seen the prize slip from the Germans' grasp as the French counter-attacked. They were to be given no such opportunity twenty-six years later. Hence the halt order of the 16th, to which Guderian had been allowed a 24-hour extension. Now, on the 17th, he was firmly told to stop. Kleist arrived by plane at Guderian's HQ at 7am and proceeded to berate his subordinate with considerable rudeness for pushing on so far, so fast. Guderian was outraged and offered his resignation, which was accepted. Luckily for Germany and Guderian, General List, Commander of the Twelfth Army, intervened on hearing the news and flying in to Guderian's HQ, patched up a compromise. He told Hurrying Heinz that the halt order had Hitler's authority behind it and must be obeyed, but he came to appreciate the state of the French and the advantage in keeping them off-balance. He ordered: 'Reconnaissance in force to be carried out. Corps Headquarters must in all circumstances remain where it is, so that it may be reached easily.'

Guderian promptly had wire laid, linking his now stationary HQ to a new mobile advanced HQ. The purpose was not to deprive the French of the chance of eavesdropping but to prevent the German High Command from finding out what he was up to.

The halt on the 17th was in fact a blessing for Guderian's troops, who were exhausted and needed sleep. Tanks needed urgent repairs. Supplies of all types needed bringing up. On the 18th the advance could be resumed.

Dunkirk and the Fall of France

The German day of rest was the day appointed by the French High Command for a counter-attack, to cut off the tortoise's head, protruding, in Churchill's colourful phrase, from its carapace. The centrepiece of the attack was the so-called 4th DCR, under Colonel de Gaulle. It was newly and only partially formed and hardly deserved to be called an armoured division. However, it was all that was available and de Gaulle had long been a proponent of the sort of warfare now being practised by the Germans. Early in the morning of the 17th just short of 100 tanks set off north-eastwards from Laon to take the strategic town of Montcornet, where the roads from St Quentin, Laon and Rheims met. It was where Guderian's force had encountered Reinhardt's 6th Panzer the previous day. The attack does not appear to have caused Guderian much concern. De Gaulle's force was heavily battered by the Luftwaffe and then pushed back by the newly arrived 10th Panzer, now released from the Stonne battlefield and assigned to guard the southern flank of Guderian's advance. Once again the Char Bs gave a good account of themselves against the German tanks and hinted at what might have been achieved with a well prepared and integrated force. French losses in men were slight but Major Bescond, the foremost specialist in the use of the Char B, was killed and twenty-three tanks lost. The attack seems to have had no impact on Guderian's plans to roll on westwards at the earliest opportunity. To the north of the German corridor fierce fighting took place in and around the Forest of Mormal. The 1st North African Division and what was left of General Prioux's light mechanised division, the 1st DLM, tried to cut into the corridor and sever the tortoise's head. They were met by 5th Panzer coming up behind Rommel's 7th. Again, as with the attacks in the south, they amounted to little more than painful reminders of what might have been with better planning and more resources.

On the 18th, at dawn, the German advance resumed. By nine o'clock the 2nd Panzer Division had seized the city of St Quentin, and just to its south, 1st Panzer was also across the Oise, rolling towards Péronne on the Somme. North of Guderian, Reinhardt's Corps pushed westwards with equal vigour and speed. Only 6th Panzer seems to have encountered any serious resistance that day, near Le Catelet, north of St Quentin. Here remnants of the 2nd DCR showed again the formidable potential of the Char B. For two-and-a-half hours the German division was held up by fierce resistance until the French, under a lieutenant-colonel, were overwhelmed by sheer numbers. The Panzers then overran the HQ of the luckless Ninth Army, battered into disintegration since its first encounters on the 14th. 10 kilometres to the north, Rommel, having advanced over 20 kilometres from Le Cateau, took Cambrai. Attacks by remnants of the 1st DLM had been treated as pinpricks. As usual, Rommel relied on speed and the impression of overwhelming force to achieve his objectives. He deliberately scattered fire from tanks and AA guns into the town's northern suburbs, his whole force throwing up great clouds of dust. As he himself later wrote:

> The enemy in Cambrai, unable in the dust to see that most of our vehicles were soft-skinned, apparently thought that a large-scale tank attack was approaching the north of the town and offered no resistance.

Panic, fear and despair were enabling German forces to win. Perhaps von Rundstedt had grasped the key fact. The French must not be allowed to recover psychologically. They must be denied a morale-boosting victory at all costs.

On the other side, de Gaulle realised just how important a victory could be for French morale. He resolved to strike north again with his 4th DCR. His losses of the 17th had been made good by reinforcement with two fresh regiments of motorised cavalry but many of his tanks were the light and obsolete R 35s. He lacked artillery support and had only one battalion of infantry. His superior, General Touchon, was sitting on the defensive with several infantry divisions, forming his newly constituted Sixth Army, guarding against a non-existent threat to Paris. De Gaulle could not persuade Touchon to release additional infantry support. Liaison with the French Air Force proved lamentable. The timing of the attack was changed without informing the would-be escorting fighters. The result was that de Gaulle's force was badly knocked about by unopposed Stukas. His force failed to penetrate across the River Serre and thereby threaten the Panzer corridor. Reluctantly, de Gaulle withdrew south behind the River Aisne, musing on what might have been had his ideas been listened to before the war and even if now, his attack had been properly supported.

Dunkirk and the Fall of France

Guderian was no more disturbed by de Gaulle's second attack than he had been by the first. He resolved to press on across the old Somme battlefield to the great target of Amiens, which in 1918 had been tantalisingly just outside the Germans' grasp. As then, it was a vital railway and supply junction, through which many of the supplies of the BEF came. For the German Panzers, Sunday the 19th was, in some ways, a day of consolidation – taking a deep breath before the final dash to the coast. Rest and resupply were necessary, even for the impatient Guderian and Rommel. The latter was forced to halt near to his newly taken prize of Cambrai. To the south Reinhardt's two divisions mopped up French resistance around Le Catelet and consolidated on the west side of the Canal du Nord, the last real obstacle before the sea. Guderian, at Péronne, prepared to dash along the north side of the River Somme but sleep for his men and petrol for his tanks had to be provided. North of Rommel, the retreat of the French from the Gembloux Gap enabled the two Panzer divisions of von Bock's Army to slip into line, creating a gigantic Panzer front of nine divisions, poised for the final throw of Manstein's plan. Only two scattered British Territorial divisions, the 12th and the 23rd, stood in the way and they were largely assigned as part of the supply chain to the bulk of the British forces further north in Belgium. They lacked divisional artillery and were quite unequal to the task of stopping the cream of the Wehrmacht.

On Monday morning the last decisive phase began at 4am: Guderian ordered 1st Panzer to take Amiens; he himself was with the lead units and reached the outskirts of the city at 8.45am, which was captured by midday. The only real defenders of Amiens were a battalion of the Royal Sussex Regiment, part of the 12th Division. They fought to the finish against the elite 1 Panzer Brigade of the 1st Panzer Division. The unit had a new commander, the heroic Balck. Under him the brigade had advanced 35 miles that morning. After seizing Amiens they moved across the Somme to gain bridgeheads on the south side, ready for the next stage in the fall of France. Guderian, after apparently undertaking a rapid tourist trip round Amiens Cathedral, went off northwards to chase up the 2nd Panzer Division and urge it on to Abbeville near the mouth of the Somme. Oberleutnant Dietz of 2nd Panzer Division later recalled the nerve-racking worries about fuel supplies:

The German Advance

The Battle Group Commander is travelling behind the lead tanks. His expression is grave. There must be something in his calculations that is not quite right. Every now and again he measures with his thumb the distance travelled against what is still to be covered. The Panzer regiments have reported that their fuel will last just as far as Abbeville. What then? What could he do with immobilised tanks outside a heavily fortified town?

The fuel supplies did just last. By 7pm Abbeville had been taken. One battalion even pushed on further to the Atlantic coast at Noyelles. By nightfall it had advanced 60 miles that day and the British and French Armies to the north were finally cut off. Guderian, not for the first time, came under aerial attack at his new HQ – this time from German planes, themselves disconcerted by the sheer speed of the advance of their own troops. German flak brought down one of the German planes. Guderian describes the event:

The crew of two floated down by parachute and were unpleasantly surprised to find me waiting for them on the ground. When the more disagreeable part of our conversation was over, I fortified the two young men with a glass of champagne.

To the north, Reinhardt's Corps moved off later and now encountered their first British troops. The 6th Panzer War Diary pays tribute to the toughness of the resistance. The British 36 Brigade, of the 12th Division, fought a hopeless but heroic defensive battle for Doullens for much of the late afternoon and evening of this momentous Monday. Its commander, Brigadier George Roupell (decorated with the Victoria Cross for exceptional gallantry in the First World War), showed a certain eccentric sang-froid. When informed that one of his battalions had been shattered by the advancing German tanks, he replied: 'Never mind the Germans. I'm just going to finish my cup of tea.' But by the end of the day the German corps had gained their objectives of Hesdin and Le Boisle and 36 Brigade had ceased to exist. Further north still, Rommel had persuaded his reluctant corps commander to allow him to launch a night advance towards Arras shortly after midnight of the 19th/20th.

Dunkirk and the Fall of France

The day did not go well. Much of Rommel's force did not keep up and the divisional commander was nearly captured by French cavalry tanks. Arras was held by British units, under Major-General Roderick Petre, Commander of 12th Division, and was not to be taken by huff and bluff as Cambrai had been. The city was reached shortly after dawn but held out all day, inflicting heavy casualties. The 7th Panzer, supported by the SS 'Totenkopf' motorised infantry division, was thrown onto the defensive and lost more men than at any time since crossing the Meuse. Petre's force was a mixed bag, its major components being the 5th Battalion of the Green Howards, the 8th Battalion Royal Northumberland Fusiliers, and from the cream of the regular British Army, the 1st Battalion Welsh Guards. Artillery was in short supply and there was a distinct shortage of official provisions. This latter problem was partially solved by the padre of the Welsh Guards, Reverend C. H. D. Cullingford, who organised effective looting raids into the abandoned shops of the city. Arras was clearly a vital strongpoint behind the main British forces to the north. Bombed repeatedly, it held out until the 24th, when the order to evacuate was received.

The British Retreat

The Allied forces in Belgium were under the overall strategic direction of the French General Billotte. On the extreme left was the French Seventh Army, which had rushed up the coast to Antwerp to aid the Dutch. It was now retreating, following the Dutch capitulation on the 14th. This left the Belgian Army, covering Brussels on the flank of the BEF. The BEF was thus sandwiched between the Belgian Army to its left and the French First Army under Blanchard on its right. Blanchard received the full weight of von Bock's thrusts and this pressure, plus the news of German breakthrough to the south, led Billotte to order a phased withdrawal on the 15th, first to the River Senne, running through Brussels, then to the River Dendre, and finally to the River Escaut. It was to be completed in three nights. This was a westward retreat of 50 miles in the face of an aggressive enemy and with the prospect of a further enemy force appearing to the rear. It was a military nightmare.

The BEF had deployed three divisions in the front line facing von Bock's forces. Next to the Belgians was II Corps, under

The British Retreat

Lieutenant-General Brooke, with 3rd Division under Montgomery in the front line by the city of Louvain, and the 4th in reserve. To their right was I Corps, under Lieutenant-General Barker. In the front line were the 1st and 2nd Divisions and the 48th was held in reserve. Four more divisions were much further back, two in general reserve (5th and 50th) and two already on the River Escaut and forming the new III Corps, under Lieutenant-General Adam (42nd and 44th). The stresses and strain of such a withdrawal were felt from top to bottom. Brooke's diary entry for the 18th records the punishing effects on himself and Barker, the two front-line corps commanders:

> I was too tired to write last night and now can barely remember what happened yesterday. The hours are so crowded and follow so fast on each other that life becomes a blur and fails to cut a groove on one's memory ...
>
> Michael Barker in a very difficult state to deal with, he is so overwrought with work and the present situation that he sees dangers where they don't exist and cannot make up his mind on any points. He is quite impossible to cooperate with. He has been worse than ever today and whenever anything is fixed he changes his mind shortly afterwards.

Barker had a nervous breakdown, as did the commander of the 2nd Division, Major-General Loyd. All ranks were dog-tired. Men marched asleep. Sometimes it was assisted by marching in threes, the two outsiders linking arms with the sleeper in the middle. Drivers fell asleep at the wheel and drove off the road or into other vehicles. The future Duke of Norfolk, then a lieutenant in Montgomery's 3rd Division, had eight hours' sleep in five days. Behind were the pursuing German troops and overhead German bombers. One Military Police corporal recalls sheltering next to two pals in a wood:

> I hadn't been in my new position ten seconds when we were straddled by three bombs. Pete had moved into my place and his brains were coming out through a hole in his tin hat and over my boots. We buried him there when it was quiet.

Dunkirk and the Fall of France

Vehicles, motorbikes and men were machine-gunned on the roads by Me 109s and Me 110s. It became second nature to dive into the nearest ditch and some developed almost a professional elegance and speed in moving from the centre of a road to lying flat in the damp bottom of a neighbouring hollow. Those without serious injury still suffered agonising blisters from the endless marching. It had only been six days since they had advanced from the French frontier and now they were returning.

All around the soldiers of the BEF was the larger civilian tragedy. Refugees of all ages filled the roads. Men, women and children abandoned their homes and their livestock. Cows were sore and bellowing for want of milking. Dogs were sometimes left chained up in deserted farms and houses, desperate for food and water. Where they were free they often attached themselves to the retreating military columns, pathetically grateful for any scraps. At times there was a surreal quality: a mobile circus was caught up in the chaos near Tournai and charging wounded elephants conjured up a picture of which Hieronymous Bosch might have been proud, when he had tried to convey an impression of hell. The gates of two lunatic asylums had also been opened releasing hundreds of their inmates into the maelstrom of misery. In this hot, sunny May, dust and smoke and the smell of burning homes never left men's nostrils.

Montgomery's 3rd Division provided almost a model of how to cope with hell. He issued the order to withdraw at 2pm. It was a manoeuvre the division had practised and in so far as anything could go like clockwork in such difficult circumstances, it did. It withdrew, as intended, through the 4th Division to the Dendre and the 4th Division then followed on the 17th. It managed the withdrawal less skilfully and lost much of its covering cavalry screen to the advancing Germans. Barker's Corps might have disintegrated under the combined disadvantage of a too rapid withdrawal of the French on their right and the dithering of Barker. The day – or days – were saved by Brooke's assiduous help and the unflappability of Major-General Alexander, commanding the 1st Division. He was ultimately to replace Barker as Barker's nervous collapse became obvious. Montgomery pulled back from the River Dendre to the Escaut in an equally exemplary manner as his first phase of withdrawal. His diary records:

The British Retreat

Disengaged in daylight.
Used artillery to effect a break-away.
Used a lot of shells.
Whole DIV back on L'Escaut line by dark.
A very tricky operation.

By the 19th, the BEF appeared to have emerged from this 'very tricky' situation in reasonable shape under the circumstances. There were now seven divisions in line on the Escaut facing east and von Bock's oncoming troops. The new line looked secure and attempts by the Germans to break in were frustrated. South of the Escaut Line, two divisions were placed in reserve, loosely linking with the garrison in Arras. But it was down here that the real problem lay. Billotte, as he constantly repeated, had no answer to the German Panzer corridor that had cut him and the BEF off. Nine German tank divisions were curling round the flank of the nine BEF divisions and it appeared that no one had an answer.

On 18 May, as the British began to settle in on the Escaut, Gort's Deputy Chief of Staff, Brigadier Sir Oliver Leese prepared the first plan for withdrawal and evacuation from Dunkirk. It was read out to Gort shortly after midnight of the 18th/19th, when he returned to HQ. The plan was a far cry from what Churchill and the War Office in London envisaged. They assumed the possibility of a breakthrough to the south to re-establish lines of supply and retain a continuous front with the French. It was cloud-cuckoo land, as the British commanders on the spot realised. General Billotte was increasingly transfixed by a sense of brooding doom, which did not inspire confidence in his British colleagues. He drove to Gort's HQ late on the night of the 18th and made a poor impression. This clearly increased Gort's susceptibility to Leese's plans for a pull back to the Channel ports. At Gort's HQ a conference of corps commanders was held on the 19th to consider the gloomy situation and it was privately agreed that Leese's plan of withdrawal to Dunkirk would be adopted if necessary, but as yet Gort did not begin serious planning for that eventuality. Nothing was said to the French on the matter. The War Office in London was, however, warned of the possibility, and that day discussions were begun with the Admiralty for evacuation under the code name 'Dynamo'. Despite an over-optimistic assessment of the true state of the French Army and a preference for a move southwards by the BEF, Churchill reluctantly issued the following decree on the morning of the 20th:

> As a precautionary measure the Admiralty should assemble a large number of small vessels in readiness to proceed to the ports and inlets on the French coast.

That same morning Churchill dispatched General 'Tiny' Ironside, Chief of the Imperial General Staff, to Gort's HQ to make sure he rejected thoughts of withdrawal and focused instead on the attack southwards. Gort pointed out the impossibility of withdrawing from engagement with one undefeated enemy – von Bock – to turn to engage another heavily armoured one, and he was faced with fast dwindling supplies. The best he could offer was a limited offensive from Arras with his two spare reserve divisions. Gort stressed doubts about his French allies and their ability to launch a joint attack with the British. Ironside began to share these doubts but asked to visit Billotte himself at the French HQ at Lens. He was appalled by what he found. Billotte and Blanchard, commander of the French First Army, 'were both in a state of complete depression'.

Ironside's nickname came from his massive 6' 4" frame and enraged at Billotte's spinelessness, shook the French general by his tunic's buttons and extracted a promise of an attack southwards towards Cambrai the next day. Ironside's fury with the French was increasingly tinged with despair with regard to the chances of the BEF: 'God help the BEF. Brought to this state by the incompetence of the French Command.'

21–23 May: 'The End Is Not Very Far Off'

The Allied High Command in Crisis

The new French commander-in-chief, General Maxime Weygand, formally took over from Gamelin on Monday the 20th but he had already cancelled Gamelin's planned counter-attack the previous day. He had arrived on the Sunday after a horrendous flight from Syria. A brief meeting with General Georges had revealed how truly desperate France's position was. Fifteen divisions had been lost as a result of the great German attack through the Ardennes and the subsequent Meuse breakout. A further forty-five, including the BEF and France's best, were threatened with capture in Belgium. The French Air Force had been pulled back south of the Aisne and had taken little part in the events of the last week. There appeared to be no reserves and munitions were running low. Relations with allies had deteriorated. Holland had capitulated and there was a distinct possibility that Belgium would do so as well. How reliable were the British? Some suspected they might cut and run. They were certainly being parsimonious, it seemed to the French, with their aircraft. Communications with Billotte and the northern French forces were difficult and had to be done via London. Weygand decided to see for himself the condition of the beleaguered French forces in the north before fixing on the exact form any counter-attack should take. He was initially going to take a train to Abbeville on the 20th but the prospect of the capture of France's commander-in-chief so horrified ministers that he was persuaded to make the trip on the 21st by air. This imposed another day's delay.

The trip on the Tuesday was fraught with setbacks and confusion. Despite a dawn departure from Le Bourget it proved difficult to gather the necessary dignitaries for the meeting, which eventually took place at Ypres. Leopold, King of the Belgians, was there waiting for Weygand when he arrived at three o'clock in the afternoon, having flown first to Béthune, then Calais, and finally been driven along choked roads to historic Ypres, only recently rebuilt after all the destruction of the First Great War. Billotte was not initially there but eventually arrived, which is more than can be said for Gort. This was unfortunate as the centrepiece of Weygand's strategic plan was to use the BEF as the spearhead of a break into the German Panzer corridor. For this to be possible, the Belgians would have to pull back to the line of the Yser, thereby abandoning most of Belgium, but massively shortening their line so that they could take over much that was held by the British, who would then be released for an offensive southwards. The king refused such a withdrawal. He was already pessimistic and saw defeat as almost inevitable. He saw no reason to sacrifice Belgium for the greater good of the alliance. He offered a partial withdrawal to the Lys, but this would not shorten the line sufficiently to release many British divisions. Weygand, under pressure of time, did not stand his ground and argue but accepted the compromise. It has been suggested that he could have appealed over the head of the Belgian king to his Government ministers who were kept waiting outside and were probably more willing to fight on. The result was a thoroughly unsatisfactory arrangement, which did not bode well for any successful counter-attack.

Since Gort had still not turned up, Weygand had to draft arrangements with Billotte. He hung on at Ypres till 7pm, hoping for Gort's presence or at least an explanation of his absence. The explanation was simple: he had not been told where Weygand was. All Gort had was a vague message from Churchill, received on the evening of the 20th: 'Weygand is coming up your way tomorrow to concert action of all forces.' Gort was eventually tracked down at his new HQ, which had just moved, and he hastened to Ypres but arrived after the French commander-in-chief had left. Weygand had been told that as all airfields had been heavily bombed, the only way back to Paris was by sea. He made his way to Dunkirk and left on a torpedo boat, which took him via Dover to Cherbourg. He remained convinced that he had been deliberately snubbed by Gort and many among the French military saw this as evidence that the British were preparing to abandon the struggle.

In fact, despite the initial exploration of evacuation, nothing had as yet been done to prepare the BEF for retreat to Dunkirk. Gort was still, despite his misgivings, prepared to accept Billotte's leadership. The failure of the French to launch an offensive on the 21st at the same time as that of the British at Arras had added to his already deep disillusion. The French attack at Cambrai went in the next day, the 22nd. Nevertheless, Gort was an honourable man and his orders from London were clear: maintain cooperation with the French. Billotte and Gort discussed the proposed new offensive late in the evening, with Gort thoroughly unconvinced of its practicality. Nothing concrete appears to have been decided other than that the British would pull back to the old frontier line, quitted eleven days before when the campaign started. Overall, Allied relations had taken another serious turn for the worse.

To round off this depressing day, the gods, once again – as so often in the campaign – seemed to favour the Germans. Driving from Ypres to see Blanchard, the French commander of the First Army, Billotte's car crashed in the darkness into a refugee lorry. The French general lingered in a coma for two days before expiring. The one man who might have coordinated a major counter-attack was gone.

The Arras Counter-Attack

The attack that Gort and Billotte had originally agreed on the 20th was to involve 4 divisions, 2 French and 2 British. General Altmayer's V Corps of the French First Army was to attack towards Cambrai at the same time as the 5th and 50th British Divisions under Major-General Franklyn around Arras thrust south into the Panzer corridor. Altmayer claimed he could not be ready until the 22nd and the only French help available on the 21st would be a flanking detachment provided by some of the battered remnants of the 3rd DLM. Gort ordered the British attack to proceed nonetheless under the field command of Major-General Martel of the 50th Division. Martel was a leading British tank expert but the only tank forces available were two battalions from the Royal Tank Regiment released from GHQ reserve. The actual attack on the 21st was by these two tank battalions, the 4th and 7th and attached, two Territorial battalions of the Durham Light Infantry from Martel's Division. The attack in other words had been considerably slimmed down. There was no air cover available as the British Air Component had been withdrawn to the UK in the light of the rapid German Panzer advance during the previous week.

In theory around 100 tanks should have been available but wear and tear along the cobbled roads and streets of Belgium had reduced these to 74. Of these 58 were Matilda Mark I infantry tanks armed only with a machine gun and capable of only 8mph. There were 16 Mark IIs, considerably faster and with a 2-pounder gun as well as a machine gun. The 2-pounder (40mm) gun had real punch, capable of knocking out all varieties of German tanks. Both were heavily armoured and impervious to the standard 37mm German anti-tank gun, also carried by the German Mark III Panzers. The Mark II Matilda in particular thus had devastating potential if used correctly and in sufficient number. Martel divided his force into two columns formed up to the north-west of the city of Arras, each column composed of a battalion of tanks and a battalion of the Durham Light Infantry. The day's objective was the River Cojeul, 6 miles to the south of the city. Martel led from the front in the style of Rommel and it was to Rommel that a real shock was delivered.

The left-hand column made up of the 7th Battalion of the RTR and the 8th Durham Light Infantry ran into the enemy at the village of Duisans less than a mile from the start point. It took prisoners and pressed on but had to leave two companies of infantry behind to hold the village and the bridge over the River Scarpe. The tanks reached the villages of Berneville and Wailly. Their initial progress was assisted by the fact that Rommel and much of the heavy armour of the 7th Panzer had pushed off to the west before the attack began. The result was that the attackers induced panic in the rear units, at times reminiscent of that in the French Ninth Army a week before. German anti-tank crews saw their shells bounce off the Matildas and some infantry began running. At Wailly the British tanks encountered the newly arrived motorised SS Division drawn from concentration camp guards and sporting the famous name of 'Totenkopf' ('Death's Head') from their skull and crossbones cap badges. Guarding and abusing unarmed prisoners was somewhat easier than dealing with invulnerable British tanks and the inexperienced Nazi soldiers broke. Many were taken prisoner by the following Durham Light Infantry. Major John King in command of a squadron of seven Matilda IIs later described an encounter with four German tanks at a roadblock. Their shells failed to penetrate the Matildas but his shells went right through them reducing two to flames. Men ran from one of the others and King and an accompanying tank under Sergeant Doyle passed through the block unscathed and proceeded to spread mayhem over several miles. The situation was only saved by mechanical breakdown of many of the Matildas and the frenzied energy of Rommel. Three of King's squadron had broken down before the battle began and this was to be repeated in many of the Matilda Is. Rommel rushed back as news of the attack reached him. He urged the use of 88mm anti-aircraft guns as anti-tank weapons and these could stop even a Matilda. He rushed from one gun position to another exhorting and encouraging and amazingly lived to tell the dramatic tale. His ADC Lieutenant Most was killed by his side yet, despite on one occasion sheltering in a shell hole in the face of a British tank he survived and the British were forced back to Warlus. The attentions of the Luftwaffe in the early evening reduced

Adolf Hitler, Reich Chancellor, Führer and Supreme Commander of the Wehrmacht. He went for broke in May 1940, his gamble paid off. (*Jupiter Images*)

Munich, September 1938: the final act of appeasement in the face of Hitler's aggressive foreign policy. (*Jupiter Images*)

French troops man the Maginot Line, a permanent network of fortifications designed to fend off the German threat. (*Jupiter Images*)

Hermann Hoth, Commander of the XV Panzer Corps. (*Jupiter Images*)

Erich Höpner, Commander of the XVI Panzer Corps. (*Jupiter Images*)

Erwin Rommel, Commander of the 7th Panzer Division. (*Jupiter Images*)

Heinz Guderian, Commander of the XIX Panzer Corps. (*Jupiter Images*)

Lord Gort, Commander of the Field Force. (*Taylor Library*)

General Billotte, Commander of Allied forces in the north, French First, Seventh, Ninth and Second, plus BEF and Belgians. (*Taylor Library*)

Major General Harold Alexander, Commander 1st Division and of the rearguard at Dunkirk. (*Taylor Library*)

Major General Bernard Montgomery, Commander of the BEF's 3rd Division. (*Taylor Library*)

Vice Admiral Bertram Ramsay. (*Taylor Library*)

Sir Hugh Dowding, Commanding Officer of RAF Fighter Command. (*Taylor Library*)

General de Gaulle, Commander French 4th Armoured Division and then Under Secretary at the War Ministry. (*Taylor Library*)

German troops cross the Meuse.
(*Jupiter Images*)

Rolling into action: German tank
deploy. (*Taylor Library*)

German 'Landsers'
goose-step into France.
(*Jupiter Images*)

French artillery battery in the Sedan sector. Much of their ammunition was captured. (*Jupiter Images*)

Columns of refugees. (*Taylor Library*)

Innocent victims: Belgian refugees.
(*Jupiter Images*)

The speed of the German advance induced panic. Here, French civilians flee the fighting carrying whatever they could.
(*Jupiter Images*)

As the refugee flood swelled, British troops advanced to take up new positions. (*Taylor Library*)

Exodus: French refugees on the road. The mass of moving citizenry slowed the French Army's advance to meet the invaders. (*Jupiter Images*)

German infantrymen follow the Panzers into action, often a long way behind. (*Taylor Library*)

German infantry assault Limburg in Belgium. (*Taylor Library*)

German artillery in action, but in numbers inferior to the French. (*Taylor Library*)

German tanks not in their natural habitat. (*Taylor Library*)

Panzers on the prowl.
(*Taylor Library*)

A German Panzer not in its natural habitat.
(*Taylor Library*)

German armour in their natural habitat pushing through open country to the Channel coast.
(*Taylor Library*)

A knocked out British light tank inspected by a German Panzer crew, but most British tanks were more heavily armoured than their German opponents. (*Taylor Library*)

'Hurrying Heinz' Guderian in an uncharacteristically static moment. (*Jupiter Images*)

SS Totenkopf troops on the march. (*Taylor Library*)

German troops march through subdued French streets. (*Taylor Library*)

Comrades-in-arms: SS Troopers and Wehrmacht Panzermen. (*Taylor Library*)

A pause in the fighting: SS troops relax. (Taylor Library)

Motorcyclists of Guderian's corps rest by the roadside. (Taylor Library)

Belgian troops lost the will to fight when news of their country's capitulation broke. (*Taylor Library*)

Churchill and Ramsay pore over maps at Dover Castle as the strategic situation across the Channel deteriorates. (*Taylor Library*)

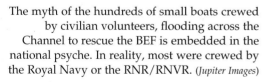

The myth of the hundreds of small boats crewed by civilian volunteers, flooding across the Channel to rescue the BEF is embedded in the national psyche. In reality, most were crewed by the Royal Navy or the RNR/RNVR. (*Jupiter Images*)

Operation Dynamo: troops queue patiently, waiting to be lifted off the Dunkirk beaches, but most were lifted from the jetty at Dunkirk itself. (*Jupiter Images*)

many ways the weather was the decisive factor in the Dunkirk evacuation, as relative calm made e loading of small boats on the beaches possible. (*Jupiter Images*)

Steadily, from 30 May, the BEF and a large element of the French First Army were removed from the Dunkirk beaches. (*Taylor Library*)

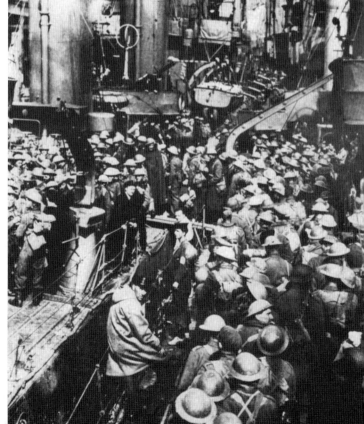

Rescued by the Navy: in all, some 224,686 soldiers of the BEF plus 141,445 Allied troops – mainly French – made it to the UK.
(*Jupiter Images*)

The survivors: exhausted British troops on their way home. (*Taylor Library*)

Homecoming heroes: British troops welcomed back from France.
(*Jupiter Images*)

Capture of the 51st
Highland Division.
(*Jupiter Images*)

Allied POWs are marched
off the beaches by their
German captors.
(*Jupiter Images*)

French POWs march into captivity. (*Taylor Library*)

British POWs file past an SS column. (*Taylor Library*)

British troops captured at Calais. (*Taylor Library*)

French POWs await their fate. (*Taylor Library*)

British corpses inspected by German orderlies. Some POWs were shot in cold blood by their SS captors. (*Taylor Library*)

The defeated: French troops, including North African units, fought a stubborn rearguard action to save the Dunkirk perimeter. (*Taylor Library*)

Wreckage of war: the French countryside following the fighting. (*Taylor Library*)

The victors: exhausted German troops relax after hard-fought battles. *(Taylor Library)*

SS warriors contemplate victory. *(Taylor Library)*

oe to the vanquished: stunned Parisians accept the inevitable. (*Jupiter Images*)

ris falls to an invasion of German tourists. (*Jupiter Images*)

Nazi Swastika flutters over the Arc de Triomphe. (*Jupiter Images*)

Going for broke pays off – the ultimate holiday snap.
(*Jupiter Images*)

The Arras Counter-Attack

the ardour of the British infantry. Lack of air cover was a debilitating handicap. After an unfortunate contretemps in which French tanks fired by mistake on their British allies, the supporting French units of the 3rd DLM assisted the British from Warlus back north to Vimy Ridge, engaging in the process in a vicious fire-fight with tanks of the 7th Panzer Division which had returned to help their stricken comrades. The 7th RTR had lost ten of its 23 Mark Is and all of the Mark IIs. The commander of the battalion, Lieutenant-Colonel Heyland, had been killed like many of his tank crews.

The attack by the left-hand column, composed of the 4th RTR, supported by the 6th Durham Light Infantry, made even further progress due south of Arras. Most of the force were Matilda Is but the battalion had been lent six Matilda IIs by the 7th Battalion to provide extra punch. Guided by a 23-year-old lieutenant, Peter Vaux, the battalion reached the start line of the Arras Doullens railway, a mile south-west of Arras. British tanks like their German enemies were equipped with radios but their reliability was far from 100 per cent. Many had had their frequencies disrupted by the jolting of the tanks on cobbled roads and communication was to be a problem throughout the battle. After crossing the railway they fanned out into a frontage of three-quarters of a mile and advanced up a slight slope. Here they encountered groups of soft-skinned German vehicles which they rapidly put out of action with little loss to themselves. As with the attacks by the other column, panic ensued in the German ranks and the following British infantry took a considerable number of prisoners. Once again it became obvious that the British tanks were impervious to German anti-tank guns and the effect was unnerving on the German columns. The British pressed on to the Cambrai road which ran along the crest of a ridge and then down a sloping hayfield towards the line of German guns on the approaching high ground. In the hayfield several of the tanks were knocked out by the German artillery. Peter Vaux who had become detached from this attack was searching for the battalion commander, and was appalled as it suddenly dawned on him viewing the hayfield that twenty or so tanks had been knocked out including that of Lieutenant-Colonel Fitzmaurice. Despite the initial success, the attack was stalling for lack of real artillery support and sufficient infantry. The battalion had given the Germans a nasty shock and inflicted considerable casualties.

Dunkirk and the Fall of France

One advanced party actually reached the village of Wancourt on the River Cojeul. But the British too had taken considerable punishment and in the evening pulled back. Vaux's account of the battle and his subsequent adventures is a wonderful testament to the sheer confusion of battle and its aftermath. Having survived combat, Vaux's light tank driver took a wrong turn on the retreat. It was dark and they were out of ammunition. They found themselves travelling too far west and at the village of Beaumetz ran into a German unit who in the dark mistook them for a German tank despite the fact that the British vehicle deliberately crashed into the back of a German lorry. They rolled on in the dark and reached Doullens, occupied by the Germans the previous day. The German traffic was heading north so they headed south towards Amiens. In effect Vaux was performing the much-vaunted British breakout to the south in one solitary light tank. When it finally ran out of petrol they were close to the Somme and had passed through most of the Panzer corridor in the night.

As the British survivors retired to Vimy Ridge, it was clear that the attack had failed to disrupt the German forces and it had cost the Royal Tank Regiment dear. Forty-six tanks had been lost, which amounted to 62 per cent of the total engaged but it had bagged large numbers of prisoners both from 7th Panzer and SS 'Totenkopf'. It had induced panic not only amongst the ordinary German soldiery but also amongst the German High Command. German commentators recorded the number of burnt-out German vehicles. Rommel talked of being attacked by hundreds of British tanks and five divisions being involved in the assault instead of the four battalions that in reality took part. Guderian in his memoirs records:

On the 21st of May a noteworthy event occurred to the north of us; English tanks attempted to break through in the direction of Paris. At Arras they came up against the SS 'Totenkopf' Division, which had not been in action before and which showed signs of panic. The English did not succeed in breaking through, but they did make a considerable impression on the Staff of Panzer Group von Kleist, which became remarkably nervous.

Operationally the attack had failed. German supply lines had not been cut. Yet strategically it did have a considerable impact. It added

The Panzers Swing North: The Battle for Boulogne

to the unease in the German High Command and contributed to the decisive mistake of 24 May, when the Panzers were halted for a crucial two days.

The French Counter-Attack of the 22nd

The French attack, which should have accompanied the British thrust south of Arras on the 21st went in at 9am on the 22nd. As with the British assault, the forces originally intended to have been used were much slimmed down. Instead of two divisions punching their way to Cambrai, a single infantry regiment of the French 25th Motorised Division with two small armoured reconnaissance groups and artillery in support formed the attacking force. The 121st Regiment demonstrated skill and courage, giving the lie to the perception that the French Army lacked these qualities. It struck the German 32nd Infantry Division and dealt it a hard blow, penetrating through to the outskirts of Cambrai. In desperation the Germans threw in obsolete squadrons of Henschel 123 bi-plane dive-bombers – a reminder that much German equipment did not outclass that of the Allies. As at Arras, it was the formidable 88mm anti-aircraft guns used in an anti-tank role at point-blank range that stopped the French. In the final resort the attack was too small-scale to be decisive and in the evening the order was given to withdraw to the start line east of Douai. A nasty shock had been administered but yet again it was too little too late.

The Panzers Swing North: The Battle for Boulogne

As the fighting to the east, around Arras and then Cambrai petered out, fresh battles developed to the west as Guderian's Panzers resumed their advance. The 21st was a day of rest for the exhausted tank divisions. Guderian was later to write it off as a wasted day that could have been profitably spent speeding northward to seize Boulogne. Late on the 21st he received orders to strike north for the Channel ports but the 10th Panzer Division was withdrawn from his corps to reinforce Rommel around Arras. Von Kleist was still nervous following the shock administered by the British attack that day. Here was one great strategic benefit from the failed British offensive. Guderian intended to use the 10th to strike for Dunkirk while the 2nd made for Boulogne and the 1st for Calais. He recorded that: 'It was with a heavy heart that I changed my plan.'

Dunkirk and the Fall of France

Dunkirk would have to wait.

In fact, the delay on the 21st served the Allies well in both Calais and Boulogne, which were virtually defenceless. The Adjutant General of the BEF, Lieutenant-General Douglas Brownrigg, had already decided to send Rear GHQ to Boulogne from Arras on 17 May. It was assumed to be safe and a more suitable base for the BEF's clerical staff. It was certainly not intended as a first step to evacuation but the French were not told of the move and it contributed to worsening relations between the Allies. However, the French planning regarding the defence of Boulogne appeared confused in the extreme. When the Rear GHQ Staff arrived the garrison was largely composed of 1,100 French naval personnel under Commandant Dutfoy de Mont de Benque. Panic appears to have been induced by rumours of approaching German armour and under pressure from his subordinates, he appears to have decided in the early hours of the 21st to evacuate the town and did so himself, going to Dunkirk. The result was chaos. Parties of drunken French sailors roamed the streets and crowded the port. Had Guderian's tanks struck north on the 21st they would have faced little opposition. By the time they did move, at 7am on the 22nd, the situation had changed. Dutfoy's superior condemned the withdrawal and ordered all French combatants to fight to the last man. A French division, the 21st, moving south to the Somme under General Lanquetot, was able to move some of its battalions to assist in the defence of the town and two British Guards battalions appeared on the 22nd fresh from the UK. It would be a scratch force holding the ancient port but it would not be the walkover that Guderian might have enjoyed on the 21st.

The Guards Brigade had been involved in a tiring night exercise near Camberley, and were less than enthusiastic about the sudden order to move to active service. Nevertheless, with commendable speed, the 2nd Irish Guards were on the quayside at Dover by 9.30pm on the 21st, ready to be loaded onto the cross-Channel ferry SS *Queen of the Channel*. The 2nd Welsh Guards were there by midnight, to be loaded onto SS *Biarritz*. Escorted by two old destroyers, one serving to carry Brigadier Fox-Pitt and brigade headquarters, the small convoy made its way across a calm sea just before dawn. A burning French oil tanker lay just offshore, reminding the new arrivals, if they needed reminding, that this was indeed active service. The port had been heavily bombed and many of the dockside buildings were now reduced to smoking rubble. Belgian, Dutch, French and British troops were milling about along with panic-stricken civilian refugees. Sailors and some of the Irish Guards had to fix bayonets to clear a passage for the disembarking soldiers. The Welsh Guards landed later, the two battalions amounting to 1,692 men. In addition there were around 1,500 members of the Auxiliary Military Pioneer Corps who had managed to struggle back to the port when the German Panzers crashed into their rear support positions on 19/20 May. Fox-Pitt faced the unenviable task of guarding a perimeter of 12 kilometres with this small force against a whole German Panzer Division. He also lacked heavy artillery and transport. Yet his orders were clear: 'Boulogne was to be held.'

The Irish Guards were deployed on a 3.5-kilometre front to the south-west of the town, and the slightly more numerous Welsh Guards on a longer front facing east. That the two battalions had time to deploy was due to the slower-than-usual progress of the 2nd Panzer Division moving north. It was not until about 3pm that the Irish first sighted isolated scout cars. The approaching Germans had encountered tough resistance from a scratch force drawn from different elements of the French 21st Division and, for once, from hostile air power. The Germans had divided their forces into two attacking groups, one heading due north and striking the southern environs of Boulogne and another further inland, destined to strike the Welsh Guards from the east. The column closest the coast ran into unexpected French defences at Nesles–Neufchatel. The French fought heroically and several German tanks were knocked out by anti-tank guns. Two more were destroyed in the more easterly advance on the road from Montreuil to Samer but by outflanking French points of resistance, German progress was continued. Guderian records that the enemy air force was very active with little interference from the Luftwaffe. In fact, seventy light bombers – Fairey Battles and Bristol Blenheims – took a toll of the Germans and emphasised how important control of the air was for an effective Blitzkrieg campaign. British aircraft were now operating from bases in southern England, while the Luftwaffe had still not effectively rebased further west. Major Freiherr von Suskind-Schwendi, commander of the 38th Panzer Jäger Battalion of the 2nd Panzer Division recorded:

> On a motorcycle with sidecar I had driven to the front to see the situation [...] Some kilometres off I saw a close formation of planes flying in the direction of our advance. Because we had hitherto only seen our own planes in close formation I thought them to be friendly too. Shortly after having seen them another commander came from behind and told me as he overtook me, that the whole staff of Tank Destroyer Battalion 38 had fallen victim to an enemy air attack. Because the situation ahead had been cleared I immediately returned – a lot of motor vehicles, among them my command car, were still burning.

Despite setbacks like this, the outskirts of Boulogne were reached. Sergeant Arthur Evans, with the anti-tank platoon of the Irish Guards, recorded the ominous rumbling of gunfire all afternoon but suddenly it grew louder and nearer and contact was made around 5pm. Half an hour later, behind a curtain of shells, the first approaching tanks were sighted. Evans recalls that:

> I could clearly see the tank commander's head above the open turret with his field glasses to his eyes. We opened fire and the tank rocked as we scored two direct hits. The crew baled out and abandoned it. Soon a second appeared and that too, was effectively disposed of.

Despite the shock of this first effective resistance, more attacks followed, particularly on the Irish Guards' left flank, where the battalion's 1st Company was dug in. Its position was slowly turned. The attacks went on after dark, the last one, at around 10pm, inflicting heavy casualties on the already strained 1st Company. All went quiet around 11pm, both sides thoroughly exhausted. Some sleep was possible but at 2.30, Colonel Haydon, the Irish Guards' battalion commander, ordered stand-to, in anticipation of a dawn attack. On the other side of the River Lianne the Welsh Guards, facing east, had an easier time. A few scout cars were sighted and

The Panzers Swing North: The Battle for Boulogne

around 6pm shelling began and the odd light tank appeared, drawing fire from the British troops. The attacks were not pressed and the Germans skirted round the Welsh Guards' position to reach the coast north of Boulogne, thus fully enveloping the city.

It was on the 23rd that the attack really began. Both Guards battalions faced continuous assault from 7.30am. The Welsh held the attacks for four hours and then began to pull back towards the quays. By two o'clock they were within 500 metres of the port and engaged in bitter rearguard actions. The Irish, likewise, faced a tough morning, this time the heaviest attacks coming on their right flank, nearest the coast, held by the 4th Company. The intensity is shown by the casualties in that company among both officers and other ranks. Of the latter, only nineteen of the original 107 survived. Between 10.30 and 11.30 Haydon ordered his men back towards the town on the west side of the river, covering the embarkation points. Bitter street fighting ensued with a horrendous din of exploding shells and almost ceaseless rifle and machine-gun fire. The Irish Guards' chaplain, assisting in a makeshift first aid post in a garage, expected the streets to be filled with both corpses and fighting soldiers, but when he risked a peep saw no one but a single young Guards officer, testimony to the apparent emptiness of a modern battlefield, swept by murderous fire. A further retreat towards the port followed at 1pm.

On the north side of the city was the Fort de La Crèche, held by French naval personnel. This was stormed at ten o'clock by the German force under Colonel von Vaerst, opening the way for a penetration south into the city. What prevented this was a scratch force of APMC soldiers under VC holder, Lieutenant-Colonel Dean, who organised his forces to build temporary barricades, barring German progress south. As one German tank started to mount and crush one such road obstacle, its gun pointing uselessly heavenwards, the barricades were doused in petrol and set alight. The tank withdrew. Dean's small force was able to shore up the left flank of the retreating Welsh.

By the middle of the afternoon a lull developed. Lying off the port were several Allied destroyers. According to one German source, these eight ships laid down a devastating fire on the attacking Germans, pumping 4.5-inch shells into their attacking columns.

Dunkirk and the Fall of France

Guderian requested Luftwaffe assistance to counter the naval gunfire and prevent the port being used. He was unsure whether the British were embarking or reinforcing their men. He may have been comforted to know that Fox-Pitt did not know either. HMS *Whitshed*, the destroyer which had brought Fox-Pitt across the previous day, now made her way into the harbour to load up civilians, refugees and APMC troops. Her guns were brought into play in the immediate vicinity. The infiltrating Germans had established a machine gun in a warehouse a mere 100 yards from *Whitshed*. Her commanding officer, Edward Condor, ordered it blown apart with two well-aimed 4.5-inch shells, eliciting a loud cheer from the Irish Guards. Their behaviour attracted favourable comment from one of *Whitshed*'s officers:

> Watching them in perfect order, moving exactly together, engaging target after target as though on parade ground drill, it was difficult to realise that this was the grim reality of battle. They were truly magnificent and no sailor who saw them could ever forget the feeling of pride he experienced.

Whitshed pulled out, fully loaded to make the crossing to Dover and her place was taken immediately by HMSs *Keith* and *Vimy*. *Keith* received a message shortly after tying up, which clarified Fox-Pitt's position. He was to evacuate. The War Office had decided that Boulogne could not be held and those troops that could be got away should be. Unfortunately, nobody informed the French and General Lanquetot in the Haute Ville was in the dark as to British intentions. Such oversights added to the growing chasm of distrust between the two allies.

Evacuation, however, was to be far from easy. At 7.30 in the evening the Luftwaffe responded dramatically to Guderian's earlier plea for help. Over sixty planes arrived, attacking both the harbour and the bombarding flotilla at sea. A modern French destroyer was sunk and the fate of those two British destroyers tied up would have been very doubtful, had not twelve Spitfires arrived almost simultaneously. The two ships loading in the harbour survived but with splinter damage. Their two captains did not. As Lieutenant-Commander Donald of *Vimy* trained his binoculars on a nearby

The Panzers Swing North: The Battle for Boulogne

hotel, from which sniper fire was coming, a bullet struck his forehead, nose and eyes. He was just able to order his first lieutenant (equivalent to a captain in the army) up to the bridge to take his place as a final order. The young sub lieutenant, also on the bridge with the ship's captain, collapsed almost at the same time with four bullets in the chest. On *Keith*, Captain David Simson, the flotilla commander, had just ordered the bridge to be cleared during the bombing raid when he too was struck by a sniper's bullet. His sub lieutenant skilfully followed *Vimy* out of Boulogne, stern first, small arms fire still rattling round the upper structures. As it pulled out, the vessel passed *Whitshed* and *Vimeira*, returning for second loads. The two that had lost their captains, with upwards of a 1,000 extra passengers, made off for Dover at top speed. The Welsh Guards were called back to the quays, crossing the Pont Marguet linking the north and south sides of the harbour before it was blown. Unfortunately, the 3rd Company could not be contacted despite the personal efforts of the battalion commander, who drove to the building they were holed up in and tried to get them to open the door.

As the reloaded *Whitshed* and *Vimeira* left, three more destroyers entered. The last, *Venetia*, took several hits, some from tanks and some from the Fort de La Crèche, where a skilled German soldier had succeeded in activating one of the supposedly disabled French guns. Crippled, with her stern blazing, she impressed the watching commander of the Welsh Guards:

> Owing to magnificent seamanship, they were able to get her out so that she wouldn't block the harbour, which is what we thought would happen. She went out stern first – blazing at the stern and with all guns firing – a magnificent sight!

The other two destroyers began to load the two Guards battalions: the Welsh onto *Venomous* and the Irish onto *Wild Swan*. The discipline impressed the watching naval officers. Just before sailing at 9.30pm the *Wild Swan* scored a direct hit on a German tank. Both ships made it back to Dover, carrying approximately 900 men each. Under cover of darkness, first HMS *Windsor* took any waiting troops, including Brigadier Fox-Pitt, and then, finally, *Vimeira* took any remnants on the quays off: these included Colonel Dean's pioneers, who had eventually made it back to the dockside. Some 4,368 had been evacuated.

Others remained. The remnants of the 3rd Company of the Welsh Guards, who had failed to get the message to retreat, made a heroic final stand in the Gare Maritime, under Major Windsor-Lewis, until Saturday, the 25th. Likewise, the French garrison fought on under General Lanquetot in the Haute Ville and Citadelle until, with the water supply cut off and ammunition and food running out, they faced an almost medieval finale. The Germans brought up two 88mm anti-aircraft guns and pulverised one section of the wall near the cathedral and then assaulted using scaling-ladders. Faced with the ultimatum that if he did not surrender, the city would be burned, Lanquetot brought the fighting to an end. It had been far from a walk-over for the 2nd Panzer Division but they had still won yet another victory.

The BEF Pulls Back from Arras and the Escaut

Gort's position was now desperate but London still did not appear to comprehend the truth. Churchill flew to Paris yet again on the 22nd and a grand strategy of counter-attack was agreed. The new French Seventh Army, south of the Somme, would strike north to Amiens as the BEF and Blanchard's First Army struck south. It was a pipe dream.

Meanwhile, Gort was in an unenviable position. He faced constant pressure on his front along the Escaut from von Bock's Army Group B. The BEF showed every intention of resisting effectively and there were no signs of the collapse that had occurred in the French Ninth Army near Sedan. Nevertheless, this was almost the least of his worries. On his left flank the Belgians were buckling under pressure from von Bock's forces and constant air attack. Gort himself could expect little air support away from the coast, now that the air combat units had pulled back to Britain. His forces in and around Arras were increasingly faced with the prospect of being cut off, as the Germans recovered from the shock of the British counter-attack and began to advance around the British salient far to the south-east of the rest of the BEF. Most worrying of all were the ominous advances of the Panzers to the south, threatening both to cut him off totally from the coast and all supply and crash into his undefended rear. To guard

24–26 May: The Beginning of a Miracle

against this disaster the 2nd and 48th Divisions were moved to hold the only real obstacle to the Panzers' advance, the La Bassée Canal and its extension, the Aa Canal. These were not enough to cover the whole area and units of Army Group A secured crossings east of St Omer. The main force of the BEF, including Montgomery's superb 3rd Division, pulled back from the Escaut Line to the old frontier defences – known as the Gort Line – on the 22nd/23rd. The troops were desperately tired and Brooke recorded that they were running short of ammunition. On the night of 23/24, the 5th and 50th Divisions around Arras were at last pulled back north – narrowly avoiding encirclement.

Brooke had begun his diary entry for the 23rd, where he wrote of supply difficulties with the even more ominous words: 'Nothing but a miracle can save the BEF now and the end cannot be very far off!'

24–26 May: The Beginning of a Miracle

Brooke did not know it but the miracle had already begun to happen. At 6pm on the 23rd, von Rundstedt ordered his Fourth Army under Kluge to halt their northern thrusts. The Panzers were to be rested and allowed to recuperate. Hitler confirmed the order the next day after visiting Rundstedt's HQ and all the armoured spearhead, including that of Kleist, were to remain south of the Aa Canal. Guderian was predictably outraged:

> We were utterly speechless. But since we were not informed of the reasons for this order, it was difficult to argue against it. The Panzer divisions were therefore instructed: Hold the line of the canal. Make use of the period of rest for general recuperation.

Guderian attributes the order to Hitler and argues that it was a decisive error that lost Germany the war. In fact the order originated with Rundstedt and was, in many ways, highly sensible. It has sometimes been argued that Hitler deliberately let the BEF off the hook in order to facilitate an easy peace. There is no convincing evidence to support this theory. Once again, the High Command was anxious for the slow-moving infantry to catch up with the 'fast units'. There still seemed the possibility that a major French counter-attack could develop from the south, as Churchill and Reynaud hoped. The

Panzers were clearly tired and their vehicles in need of repair. The three divisions within XXXIX Corps (two Panzer divisions and one motorised division) had each lost an average of fifty officers and 1,500 men. A third of their tanks were out of action, as were many guns. Guderian's own 2nd and 10th Panzers were heavily – and apparently expensively – engaged in assaulting Boulogne and Calais, without, as yet, decisive results. The Panzers would be needed for the eventual swing south to defeat the rest of the French Army and the BEF, and the trapped French First Army could be finished off by a combination of von Bock's Army Group B and the Luftwaffe. In fact, the latter would find their task easier if there were not constant problems in identifying targets and sorting friend from foe. If the German Panzers proceeded north of the Aa, then many more of the friendly fire incidents that had already occurred would be repeated.

What enabled the British to capitalise effectively on this stroke of luck was the crucial decision, taken by Gort on the 25th, which would save the BEF. He decided to abandon any hope of counter-attack and breakout to the south and pull back to Dunkirk and its surrounding coast. Lieutenant General Adam of III Corps was told to relinquish his corps, take command of Dunkirk, and establish a perimeter defence into which the BEF would withdraw. The two 'spare' divisions pulled back from Arras and originally scheduled as part of the British thrust south would now be used to defend the increasingly fragile corridor down which the BEF would have to retreat. The 5th was ordered north to hold a crucial 10-mile line from Ypres to Commines. Here the collapse of the Belgian Army threatened to enable von Bock to envelop the British forces facing eastwards, cutting off their line of retreat.

On the 25th, however, the British enjoyed another stroke of luck. A British patrol from the 3rd Division had crossed the Lys and encountered a German staff car: Sergeant Burford of the Middlesex Regiment killed the driver and following the crash, the passenger, a German lieutenant-colonel, leapt out, leaving his briefcase behind. Burford seized the case and made it back to British lines. The case contained plans dated the 24th for the latest German assault by von Bock's Army Group on the hapless Belgians and the BEF.

Meanwhile, the 50th Division would also have to be used to defend the northern flank and it was moved into line north of Ypres on the 27th along the Yser Canal. Behind the shield provided by the 5th and 50th Divisions Brooke's Corps would retreat from the frontier defences they had reached on the 23rd, back to the Lys, and then north-westwards to the coast. The German halt order on Gort's southern front was put to good use in garrisoning strongpoints behind the La Bassée–Aa Canal. Many of the men came from a brigade under acting Brigadier The Hon. N. F. Somerset of the 48th Division. They were told to proceed to the beautiful little town of Cassel, sitting on one of the few hills in the area and a key nodal point. It had already entered national folklore as the hill up which the Grand Old Duke of York had marched his 10,000 men in the 1790s. Somerset had somewhat less than 10,000 but intended that his occupation would be less futile than that of the Duke of York. The defence of such centres in the next few days was to be crucial in keeping open the corridor of retreat.

On Sunday the 26th the Government in London reached the same conclusion as Gort. It had dawned on Churchill and the War Office that the vaunted French offensive from the south was not going to happen and the imminent collapse of the Belgian Army threatened disaster. Anthony Eden, the War Minister, dispatched a gloomy message to Gort early on the 26th:

> In such conditions only course open to you may be to fight your way back to west where all beaches and ports east of Gravelines will be used for embarkation.

The sudden realisation of the seriousness of the situation in London is wonderfully captured in the diary of John Colville, Churchill's secretary. It also reveals how much of the relaxed Governmental attitudes of the pre-war world survived. Colville had been given the weekend off and went to Oxford, spending an enjoyable two days walking in Christchurch Meadows, dining at *The Trout*, and discussing the merits of Socialism. On his return on Monday morning, he records:

> At Downing Street I was distressed to find the situation much blacker than when I left on Friday. It appears that a grave deterioration has taken place in the last forty-eight hours: the

BEF, unable to force their way southwards, have got to retreat to the coast as best they can and re-embark for England from whatever Channel ports remain open to them. The French seem demoralised and there is now serious fear that they may collapse. The Cabinet are feverishly considering our ability to carry on the war in such circumstances.

The Siege of Calais

While Colville was taking time off in Oxford, a heroic tragedy was being played out just across the Channel, and his boss was the direct author of these events. The bitter fight for Calais is still the subject of controversy. Did Churchill needlessly sacrifice fine and much needed soldiers in a futile gesture or was it a key contributor to the eventual success of the extrication of the BEF? Churchill, not surprisingly, argued that it was vital:

> Calais was the crux. Many other causes might have prevented the deliverance of Dunkirk, but it is certain that the three days gained by the defence of Calais enabled the Gravelines waterline to be held and without this, even in spite of Hitler's vacillations and Rundstedt's orders, all would have been cut off and lost.

Others, including Guderian, have seen it as an irrelevance. Certainly one of the motives in keeping troops in Calais and refusing to evacuate them was to placate the French and to try to undo some of the suspicion and distrust engendered by the withdrawal from Boulogne. Whether it was a vital strategic action or a political gesture, many died as a result of the decision to cling on to Calais. Perhaps such controversies are inevitable given the pressures of the hurly-burly of war.

The first forces to be sent to this old possession of England, which had been lost in the winter of 1557–1558 were two units: the 3rd Battalion Royal Tank Regiment was sent from Dover on the 22nd, without its tanks, which were dispatched separately. At the same time an understrength Territorial battalion, the Queen Victoria Rifles, was also dispatched. The port had been bombed – and was being bombed – so badly in fact, the ship transporting the tanks from Southampton wished to leave without unloading. The none-too-subtle pressure of a revolver pressed to the captain's chest ensured that the tanks were reunited with their users. Next day, the 23rd, these two units were joined by 2nd Battalion King's Royal Rifle Corps (Green Jackets) and 1st Battalion the Rifle Brigade. The whole was commanded by Brigadier Claude Nicholson. It was a valuable force and should have been a key component in the 1st British Armoured Division. It lacked artillery and other key supplies, such as demolition charges, and the Rifle Brigade lacked many of their allotted carriers, which were not unloaded. Despite bravery and skill it was not likely to prove a match for a whole Panzer division.

Furthermore, Nicholson's orders appeared confused and contradictory. There was talk of relieving Boulogne then priority orders to escort supplies north to Dunkirk were received, despite the presence of another Panzer division in the way. On the 23rd the 10th Panzer Division was ordered to take Calais and Nicholson found himself surrounded. It was still not clear what they were to do. In the early hours of the 24th a telegram was received from the War Office indicating that evacuation had been agreed in principle. In the course of the 24th bitter fighting occurred as the Germans pushed the British riflemen back – but at considerable cost to themselves. The difficulty of the struggle was causing the German divisional commander qualms, but the massive earthen ramparts of Vauban (the brilliant fortification expert of Louis XIV in the seventeenth century) weakened the impact of bombing and there appeared to be no alternative to continuing with frontal assaults. The Germans made slow and costly progress. Evacuation was planned for the 25th but French protests intervened and London decided to uphold the command to Nicholson from his nominal French superior, General Fagalde (recently appointed as commander of all Allied troops in Channel ports) to fight on. There was even confusion in the telegrams sent from the War Office. The first one, confirming the order of Fagalde, spoke of the need to uphold Allied solidarity but admitted that the port of Calais was of little importance now to the BEF. In other words, it was almost admitting to Nicholson that the Government required a futile gesture – hardly the most effective way to inspire heroic sacrifice. Churchill was not surprisingly displeased with its tone and had a second sent at 2pm redolent with patriotic bombast:

Dunkirk and the Fall of France

> The eyes of the Empire are upon the defence of Calais, and His Majesty's Government are confident that you and your gallant Regiment will perform an exploit worthy of the British name.

Long before the telegram was received, Nicholson's forces had been fighting ferociously against a series of major assaults, which had begun at sunrise. Lacking artillery, the riflemen – probably the best marksmen in any army – directed a formidable small-arms fire at the attacking infantry when the German artillery barrage lifted. The British retreated to an inner perimeter inside the old town and the Germans were able to capture the *Hotel De Ville*. In an attempt to minimise his own casualties, as well as the British, the German commander invited Nicholson via the agency of the French mayor, to surrender at 9am on the 25th: 'No, I shall not surrender. Tell the Germans that if they want Calais they will have to fight for it,' came the reply. Bitter fighting resumed.

A further request for surrender was sent during the afternoon, this time through a German officer, to whom the famous answer was returned: 'The answer is no, as it is the British Army's duty to fight as well as it is the German's.'

Heavy artillery brought up from Boulogne was now used to pour shells into the old city. The suffering of individual soldiers was horrific yet resistance continued, as it did from the French garrison in the citadel. Their ageing commander was to die of a heart attack on the next day. At 6.30pm the Germans tried to seize the three bridges into the old town, beginning with a hurricane artillery barrage. Half an hour later, as the barrage stopped, two attacks on two of the bridges were driven back and the supporting German tanks knocked out. That on the third bridge temporarily succeeded but a counter-attack by the 60th threw them back. The attacks died away at nightfall, both sides exhausted.

Fresh attacks began at 7am with artillery bombardment followed by infantry assaults. The Luftwaffe now added a further heavy dose of high explosive followed by ninety minutes of artillery fire. At midday heavy attacks developed on the bridges behind a creeping mortar barrage. This time the Germans succeeded and the British forces were split, some in the citadel and others cut off in the docks area. Nicholson himself was eventually surrounded and taken prisoner at around 3pm. Sporadic fighting slowly died away late on the 26th. The last to surrender were a decimated company of the Queen Victoria Rifles. The part-time soldiers, commanded by the bursar of a London University College, had equalled the regulars in bravery and determination. Despite the prohibition on a general evacuation the motorised yacht *Gulzar* lifted off a remnant under cover of darkness from a pier. The battle for Calais had ended. The battle for Dunkirk was about to begin.

27–29 May: Retreat and Evacuation

The Breakdown of Allied Cooperation

The accidental death of Billotte added to the inevitable strains under which the coalition worked. Blanchard, his successor, was unable to impose any real coordination on the three armies, which even in the happier circumstances of two weeks earlier, had tended to operate as three separate entities. Now, under the impact of repeated hammer blows from two vastly superior German Army Groups, almost total disintegration took place. As already indicated above, Gort had resolved on the 25th to save the BEF and the British War Cabinet had endorsed his decision on the 26th. Blanchard was not informed of this until the 28th, when he was duly horrified. His horror at this latest British betrayal was only somewhat modified by his even greater horror at the Belgian capitulation in the early hours of that day. In fact, the Belgian surrender should not have been unexpected. Some British commanders had expected it sooner, for King Leopold and the Belgian High Command had been hinting for some time that they could not carry on. Their decision on the 27th to ask the Germans for an armistice was not unreasonable. They had lost most of the country, including the capital, and 450,000 troops were now crowded into a western segment. Many soldiers were exhausted, ammunition was running out and food was short. In his memoirs of 1947, the Belgian Chief of Staff, General Michiels, gave an effective defence of the decision he supported at the time:

> In a space of 1,700 square kilometres between our front, the Yser, and the sea were crowded 450,000 troops, a flood of 800,000 inhabitants and an equal number of refugees. It was in the midst

93

of these bewildered people that the Germans would have pursued their attack. They as well as the troops would have been mown down. Without procuring the least advantage to our allies [...] It was to avoid this useless effusion of blood that the King decided about 4.30pm to send an envoy to the German Command.

The suffering of civilians was manifest. On the day the Belgians requested a ceasefire an appalling massacre of Belgian civilians had been carried out by one German regiment of the 225th Division at the village of Vinkt. The area had been the scene of ferocious resistance to the German attackers by the crack Belgian Chasseurs Ardennais, who had inflicted heavy casualties on the Germans before retreating. Farms were subsequently ransacked and the inhabitants butchered. Worst of all, on the afternoon of the 28th, inhabitants of the village were forced to watch the execution of selected males. The innocent villagers were told not to avert their eyes from the shootings on pain themselves of being shot. Seventy-eight civilians appear to have been killed in a series of incidents in and around the village, the eldest being a man of eighty-nine.

Leopold and many of his advisers clearly felt that nothing was to be gained by further resistance. The British were about to leave and French counter-attacks had apparently evaporated. Belgium, it appeared, was fighting simply to allow her allies to escape. No word, however, was passed to Blanchard of the timing of the surrender, which came into effect at 4am on the 28th. This was, of course, a potential disaster for the British, making possible a German thrust along the coast to Nieuport and Dunkirk. Little stood in the way of von Bock's forces.

The French First Army, the finest and best equipped, was stuck to the east of the BEF between Béthune and Lille. At first, Blanchard would not countenance withdrawal other than to the Lys, and by the time the order was given to pull back with the BEF, late on the 28th, it was too late to save the whole army. By this time a thrust north over the La Bassée Canal by Rommel's 7th Panzer, acting with the 5th (also under his control) had broken through after hard fighting on the 27th. Rommel then swung north-east to link with von Bock's southward advancing infantry, thereby cutting off five divisions of the First Army around Lille. Their new commander, General Prioux, was captured next day, but under General Molinie, the isolated corps fought on in a desperate but hopeless struggle against superior German forces. Seven German divisions, three of them Panzers, battered the French into eventual submission at Lille late on the 31st. This heroic final stand made 'a splendid contribution', in Churchill's words, to the escape of the BEF and some of the First Army. Prominent among the defenders were North African troops.

Saving the BEF

Despite the unlooked-for good fortune of the German halt order of the 24th and the capture of German plans on the 25th, the BEF's situation still looked bleak in the extreme on the 27th. Colville was right to point up the black nature of that Monday morning. True, strongpoints had been established along the southern flank, while the Panzers were held back. True, a firmer northern flank had been established from Ypres to Commines and true, some units of the French Army had begun pulling back to the Lys with the BEF (but nearly two corps had been cut off in Lille). Nevertheless, the prospects were not good. Over 300,000 troops were strung out along a 60-mile corridor, threatened from north and south by a vastly superior enemy who enjoyed total command of the air. Supplies were increasingly difficult and on the northern flank of the BEF, the collapse of the Belgian Army in the early hours of the 28th – later than Gort and Brooke feared – still raised the terrifying prospect that von Bock's divisions could sweep round the north-west flank of the BEF into Nieuport and Dunkirk. What must be appreciated is the sheer difficulty and danger of retreat in the face of a superior enemy with high morale and plenty of aggression. What is amazing is the quality of the performance of the BEF in the most difficult of situations. In this sense it was the finest hour of the British Army – much more impressive than its, at times, lack-lustre advance in France and Belgium four years later, as the junior ally of the USA.

The handling of the northern flank was a military triumph for Brooke and his divisional commanders, particularly Montgomery and Franklyn. Little in the hard fighting and manoeuvres of these days suggests the superiority of the Wehrmacht. Franklyn's 5th Division, only two brigades strong, was given extensive artillery support and various reinforcements from other units skilfully fed in by Brooke. The line was held and the Battle of Wytschaete over the three days 25–28 May deserves better recognition as a military victory, as Franklyn successfully resisted far superior forces. The artillery lent by I Corps was particularly effective in breaking up German attacks, firing 5,000 rounds in thirty-six hours. It was only in the bombardment preceding El Alamein that this intensity was exceeded. Nor was the defence merely static or reliant on weight of artillery. On Monday evening Franklyn launched a highly effective counter-attack using the two battalions loaned from the 1st Division, the Grenadiers and the North Staffordshires, which knocked the enemy off-balance and stabilised the line. The War Diary of the German IV Corps was particularly complimentary to the defensive skills of the BEF after the battle. On the night of 28–29 Franklyn disengaged his forces. This was a difficult and costly manoeuvre for individual units, such as the 2nd Royal Scots Fusiliers. The remnants of his two brigades swung back from confrontation and then retreated north through a defensive line formed by the 3rd and 4th Divisions between Ypres and Poperinghe. These divisions themselves had only been able to pull back from their extended position south-east of Menin because of the cover provided to their flank by Franklyn's force.

Montgomery was ordered to perform a particularly difficult task in withdrawing at night behind the 5th Division to take up a position north of Ypres. It was a remarkably complex task to accomplish. Contact with an enemy had to be broken off, although this was helped by the capture of the German attack plans on the 25th. Two rivers had to be crossed, the Deule and the Lys, and a 20-mile journey at night by minor roads made to take up dawn positions along the Yser Canal against a new enemy. Brooke was full of praise for his divisional commander:

> Proceeded further north to see whether Monty had reached his front along canal north of Ypres. Found he had as usual accomplished almost the impossible and had marched from Roubaix to north of Ypres, a flank march past front of attack, and was firmly established in line with French DLM to his north.

Saving the BEF

The whole episode resembles a remarkably skilful ballet, orchestrated by Brooke and made possible by the bravery and professionalism of the ordinary British soldier.

Even with the 3rd Division in place north of Ypres, there was still a gaping hole of 18 miles left by the collapse of the Belgian Army. The River Yser, running north, formed a natural barrier, but even natural barriers require manning and there were insufficient troops available. Thrusting into the gap were two German divisions: the 216th to the Yser crossing at Dixmude and directly at Nieuport; the 256th to the northern end of the Dunkirk beachhead. These were but the advance guards of two whole German armies, the Sixth and the Eighteenth. Should either or both of these German units succeed in crossing the river the whole BEF, other than the small numbers already around Dunkirk, would be cut off. Initially, all that was available was a screening force provided by the 12th Lancers and their armoured cars. In addition, there were the struggling remnants of a battered French DLM and the French 60th Infantry Division, which had been attached to the Belgian Army. As it tried to withdraw, many of its men were overrun by the advancing Germans and forced to surrender. It was a desperate race against time, the British struggling to blow all the bridges over the Yser before the Germans could seize them. The chaos of the swarming refugees, the retreating French 60th and even the weather, which now turned wet, slowed up the Germans. One of the British heroes of this phase was a twenty-six-year-old lieutenant of the Royal Engineers, David Smith. After blowing up the main bridge near Ypres' Menin Gate late on the afternoon of the 27th, he proceeded on the 28th to blow a series of bridges to the north, all the way to Dixmude. No sooner had the bridge been blown than a column of German motorcyclists appeared, followed by 250 lorries bearing German troops. Four armoured cars of the 12th Lancers faced them. These were reinforced just in time and the same situation was repeated further north all along the Yser. The corridor's northern flank was held – just.

The greatest crisis developed at Nieuport. A scratch force to defend the perimeter had been improvised by Adam and the divisional artillery commander of the 48th Division, Brigadier E. F. Lawson. He and another brigadier, Clifton, appointed to take charge of the area around Nieuport, had assembled a mixed force of artillerymen and engineers on the 28th to hold the town against a force of German motorcyclists. But a vicious fight for the bridges developed, with the British artillerymen and engineers fighting as infantry against an ever-growing force of Germans with an increasing quantity of artillery. The 4th Division of Brooke's II Corps was designated to hold this northern end of the Dunkirk perimeter. It only left the River Lys at 9pm on the 28th. Passing through Poperinghe at 5am, it was not until 10am on the 29th that the first advanced forces arrived at the threatened town. Gradually, late on the 29th, the 2nd Royal Fusiliers and the 1st Battalion of the South Lancashire Regiment deployed for action and threw the Germans back, securing the canal banks. Once again it had been touch-and-go but a combination of luck and determination prevailed.

Defence of the Southern Flank

The German halt order of the 24th had made possible the creation of a defensive line initially along the line of the La Bassée–Aa–Gravelines canal line, but then, behind this, various strongpoints were established and manned, such as those at Cassel and Hazebrouck. Perhaps the most difficult position was that held by the 2nd Division at the far south-east of the line. They would have the furthest to retreat and were being asked to cover a 20-mile front, which after retreat from the canal could leave them stranded in open country facing tanks – and there were plenty of tanks. Opposing them were no less than four Panzer divisions and two motorised SS infantry divisions. North of the 2nd Division was the 44th (Home Counties) Division and north of them the 48th (South Midland) Division. Facing these British defenders were two more Panzer divisions, supported by three infantry divisions. It looked a most unequal fight.

The halt order was lifted on the 26th and the 2nd Division was subjected to heavy artillery fire and probing infantry attacks. In La Bassée itself, the 1st Queen's Own Cameron Highlanders, at the extreme end of the line, set a magnificent example, holding out for two days to the 28th. One company was reduced to six men. Only seventy-nine of the entire battalion were to make it back to Britain. Further north and west, the 2nd Royal Norfolks held the line. They were to be pushed back to make a stand on the 27th around the village of Le Paradis. The Headquarters Company was cut off and, surrounded and running out of ammunition, were unfortunate enough to surrender to a company of the SS 'Totenkopf' Division. This German unit suffered heavily in the fighting, and drawn from concentration camp guards – unaccustomed to any resistance from the unarmed victims they were used to tormenting – now took a brutal revenge on the English soldiers who had given them such a hard time. Two of the British prisoners miraculously survived and provided testimony to the brutality of the treatment meted out by the SS men. Signaller Bert Pooley was already wounded when they surrendered. He was invited to sit but promptly kicked in the ribs when he did. Four teeth were knocked out when he looked reprovingly at a guard who had pinched his cigarettes. Harsh as this may appear, it was as nothing compared with what was to follow. All the prisoners were marched some distance to another farm and lined up in front of a pit with two machine guns trained on them. Pooley received only a flesh wound but fell. The machine guns stopped firing and the horror of hearing bayonets fixed and pistol shots indicated the process of finishing off the wounded. Just as he felt he was about to be given the coup de grâce and suffering two bullets in the leg as a German fired at a twitching body close by, a whistle blew and the SS withdrew. Another signaller also survived, both to be taken prisoner shortly afterwards by the regular Wehrmacht. The evidence of Pooley later ensured the conviction and hanging of the SS Company Commander, Fritz Knöchlein, in 1949.

Elsewhere, men of the 2nd Division also fought with heroic determination against overwhelming odds. The 2nd Dorsets at Festubert, just north of the canal grimly clung on to their position and at Merville, the 1st Royal Scots held up another SS division's advance at the Lys crossing, at enormous cost to itself. The battalion was reduced to company strength and when finally forced to surrender on the 27th, it seemed they would meet the same fate as the Royal Norfolks at Le Paradis. The pleas of the chaplain saved the wounded and a passing senior Wehrmacht officer stopped the SS from shooting other prisoners just in the nick of time as they were being lined up for execution. Early on the 28th General Irwin decided that his division had done all that could be expected of it and prepared to retreat with the surviving remnants to Dunkirk.

Dunkirk and the Fall of France

Further north the same pattern of courageous resistance and SS brutality was repeated. At Cassel, the 2nd Gloucesters (Glosters) and the 4th Oxford and Buckinghamshire Light Infantry had dug in and been told to hold. The two battalions established their HQs in the town, the Glosters in the Bank and the 'Ox and Bucks' in the *Gendarmerie*. Three strongpoints were established outside the town to break up any approaching attack. Two were overrun on the 27th but a blockhouse $2\frac{1}{2}$ miles to the north, manned by a platoon of the Glosters under Lieutenant Cresswell, held out till the 30th, despite lack of supplies and facing a fire in the building for the last thirty-six hours. The town itself was repeatedly bombed and shelled and subjected to infantry and tank assault. A ferocious attack on the 27th was beaten off. The 28th was quieter, with the Germans seeking to move round the obstacle. On the 29th renewed attacks began, this time from three sides. The order was also received to withdraw when possible. The brigadier decided to wait until night to effect a breakout. Most were to be killed, wounded or captured, but small groups – like that of thirteen men under nineteen-year-old Second Lieutenant Fane – made it to Dunkirk. Fane enjoyed considerable luck but also showed real leadership and initiative, on one occasion asking the way in the dark from a German. They reached the Dunkirk perimeter on 2 June, a Sunday.

North of Cassel, another unit of the 48th Division was in place guarding another strongpoint. The 2nd Battalion the Royal Warwickshire Regiment took up position in Wormhout on Sunday, the 26th. Bitter fighting took place on the 27th and again, during the afternoon of the 28th, against troops of the SS 'Leibstandarte Adolf Hitler'. Once again brutal disregard for the Geneva Convention was the order of the day. Individual prisoners were subjected to shootings and beatings in and around the town. The worst incident occurred when one platoon, virtually out of ammunition and facing approaching tanks, surrendered and were marched off towards a barn, half a mile from the road, where they had been captured. This was not to provide shelter from the pouring rain. Herded inside, grenades were then tossed in and thereafter survivors were ordered out in fives to be shot. Several actually survived to be taken into custody by regular troops. Despite the evidence of these survivors nobody was convicted for the atrocity after the war. Some of the defenders of Wormhout were able to withdraw late on the 28th and eventually made it back to Dunkirk, at times using bayonets in hand-to-hand combat. However, only seven officers and 130 men out of the entire battalion made such an escape.

Slowly, the Germans of Army Group A pushed north from the canal line, taking strongpoint after strongpoint but only after bitter struggles. The rain on the 28th slowed down the German tanks. The weather, which had so favoured the attackers throughout the campaign, now favoured the defender. Gradually, the British divisions pulled back towards the Dunkirk perimeter. Those like the battered brigades of the 2nd Division and the scattered garrisons of the 48th and 44th Divisions often in small groups. Units of the 42nd Division fought a dogged battle near the Yser on the 29th but by this time most of the surviving BEF was united and either within the defence perimeter or close to it. Alexander's 1st Division had been the first to arrive and with the 3rd and 4th of Brooke's Corps was the least damaged, although battalions had been detached to prop up Franklyn's small 5th Division on the Ypres–Commines front. Brooke recorded that on the 30th, 3rd Division was still 13,000-strong and the 4th 12,000. This could not be said for the battered 2nd, which had almost ceased to exist, nor for the 5th, whose two brigades were down to 600 men each.

The retreat was a remarkable achievement. Luck had played a part but the BEF had fought magnificently. The sufferings of individual wounded soldiers were horrendous and even those not wounded record the discomfort. Private Fred Clapham of the Durham Light Infantry recalls:

> The weather was very hot and sunny all the time that we were walking to the coast. As we were all wearing army issue woollen 'long johns', our crotches were all sore with constant rubbing of the garments and perspiration. Consequently, after a few days, we were marching with our legs as far apart as we could, officers included. It must have looked quite comical.

Perhaps with this in mind the downpour of the 28th was doubly welcome. The German Army had found the BEF a tough nut to crack and its tank losses from this period bear witness to the difficulty of the fighting, much of it, unlike the previous ten days, against the BEF. A total of 485 tanks were lost between the 21st and 31st, compared with 127 in the first ten days of the campaign.

The Evacuation Begins

Clearly one precondition for the BEF's escape was that it should reach the coast – and a part of the coast from which men could be embarked. Dunkirk and the miles of sandy beaches around were in some ways ideal, in others not. On the plus side, the beaches to the north of Dunkirk could, at a pinch, be used to lift men off if the sea was calm. Gently sloping sand stretched for 16 miles all the way to Nieuport Bains at the northern end of the chosen refuge. Both the beaches and the sand dunes behind, which together stretched back from the sea for a mile, provided an excellent assembly area for over a quarter of a million exhausted soldiers. The sand dunes could easily be transformed to provide shallow dugouts, which would limit the effects of bombs or artillery bombardment. Little resorts were dotted along the seafront providing natural control centres. The resort of La Panne, selected by Adam as the site of his HQ, had the major advantage of a direct undersea telephone link to England. This fortuitous circumstance arose because La Panne was the site of the Belgian king's holiday villa and he liked to keep in touch with the London Stock Exchange for the better management of his investments. Dunkirk itself was a major port but all the main harbour area was out of action from the 20th, following heavy bombing. This left two extraordinary structures, two long wooden jetties that stretched out to sea. The Jetée de l'Est, usually known by its English name, the East Mole, was 1,400 yards long and no more than 5 feet wide. Along this slender pathway, salvation or at least the opportunity of reaching England was to lie for thousands of soldiers. In addition to these possible advantages, the whole assembly area could be defended in depth. The chosen perimeter up to 3 miles from the eastern beaches and 7 miles from Dunkirk and its immediately adjacent seafront ran along a canal and there were other canals and waterways plus deliberately flooded areas, which would impede any attacker – particularly tanks.

On the negative side, there were strong tidal currents that made Dunkirk a difficult harbour to use at the best of times. Furthermore,

The Evacuation Begins

it was impossible simply to leave Dunkirk and sail for England by the most direct route. A large sandbank prevented this. The normal method of reaching the Kent coast involved a sharp turn to port on leaving Dunkirk and a sail along the French coast along a deep water channel till near to Calais when another turn, this time to starboard (the right), enabled ships to cross the Channel to Dover. This journey was some 39 sea miles. Unfortunately, this passed close to Gravelines with its heavy artillery batteries. From the 26th these were in German hands. Two other routes were possible: one dangerously across the sandbank of 55 miles, and a most indirect – but safer – route, which involved turning first east then north and finally turning towards Ramsgate via the Goodwin Lightship, only reaching Dover after a journey of 87 sea miles.

The problems were not insoluble but required skill and knowledge. Such qualities were not in short supply in His Majesty's Royal Navy and it was the RN's professional expertise that was the key ingredient in the success of the evacuation. As early as 14 May, long before defeat and retreat in Flanders had been contemplated, the Admiralty requested that all boat owners of craft between 30 and 100 feet long be registered. On the 19th, as indicated above, planning began for a possible evacuation and the task was assigned to Vice-Admiral Sir Bertram Ramsay, flag-officer in command of Dover. The ships immediately available were insufficient to lift more than 10,000 per day from each of the three Channel ports, but of course, by the 26th only one of the three ports was left in Allied hands ... Ramsay began to acquire more shipping. Thirty passenger ferries, twelve drifters, six coasters and on the 22nd, forty Dutch *schuits*, which had escaped to England. These were flat-bottomed transporters with a small draught – well suited to the shallow waters around Dunkirk. Their new Royal Navy crews christened them 'skoots'. The most valuable of the ships available were the destroyers of the Navy. Of approximately 1,000 tons these, although not comfortable as passenger ships, were fast and able to offer some anti-aircraft protection, while carrying around 600 or more soldiers to safety. Destroyers were in short supply and those Ramsay had were battered and served by crews already exhausted by the withdrawals from Boulogne and the fight at Calais.

At 18.57, on Sunday 26th, Ramsay received the signal to begin Operation Dynamo. He had 130 requisitioned merchant ships available by this time, in addition to Royal Naval craft. Already in excess of 27,000 had been evacuated, largely wounded and non-combatants. Gathering the fleet was only part of Ramsay's efficient preparations. A dedicated Staff had been assembled around him in the underground offices at Dover Castle. The choice of the code name for the whole operation arose as one of the central rooms of the command had housed an electrical generator. Captain William Tennant was to go to Dunkirk with a large team of over 150 to supervise the embarkation. A skilled hydrographer, Commander A. Day, worked out routes and Rear-Admiral Wake-Walker was appointed to command shipping off the coast of Dunkirk. In England considerable thought was given to transportation and dispersal from the landing points: 186 trains were assembled from all the different regions, forty from Great Western joined forty-seven from LNER and forty-four from LMS. Fifty-five special trains moved evacuees between the 20th and 26th and difficulties were assessed and ironed out. London was to be avoided as a possible congestion point. As Ramsay launched the operation it was hoped that over the two or three days – the only time expected to be available – perhaps 45,000 at most might be saved. It was assumed these would be largely taken from the beaches.

The loading on the 27th was slow, with small boats taking considerable time to fill their mother crafts waiting offshore in the deeper water of the Dunkirk channel or 'Rade de Dunkerque'. The day became known as 'Bloody Monday' from the extensive attention given the city by the Luftwaffe. The short-range Stukas could be rebased closer to the embarkation area and now joined Heinkels, Dorniers and Junkers 88s in plastering the port. Captain Tennant and his team crossed in the destroyer *Wolfhound* and found themselves continuously attacked but arrived unharmed. Scenes of chaos and disorder greeted them. Front-line units, for the most part, had yet to arrive and the town was partly filled with parties of ill-disciplined rear units and some deserters. Many of the tales of discipline breaking down date from this early period. The bombing put an end to any hope of using the regular dock facilities. A mere 7,669 were rescued that day but late on Tennant surveyed the two moles and noted they had escaped unscathed from the bombing. He decided to try to use the East Mole for embarkation. A passenger steamer was ordered to attempt to tie up. It did so and in under an hour had loaded 950 men. The future brightened.

On Tuesday the 28th, 11,874 were lifted from the mole, compared with 5,930 from the beaches. It was found possible to load a destroyer with 600 men in twenty minutes and then be off. It required seamanship to berth and great skill to leave, exiting astern, but these were skills the Navy possessed. It required considerable courage to embark. Temporary gangplanks and ladders linked the vessels to the pier and the tide could raise or lower the ships as much as 16 feet. Tight discipline was needed in assembling and directing the troops first onto the jetty and then into the appropriate ship. Commander Clouston was appointed pier master and was clearly prepared to use his side-arm to enforce discipline, as were his assistants. One over-eager evacuee who refused to obey commands was promptly shot dead by a naval lieutenant. This was a far cry from a world that attempts to enforce discipline by the use of ASBOs. Ramsay received considerable reinforcements this day with the addition of an anti-aircraft cruiser and a large increase in destroyers, many of them very modern and fast. Thirty destroyers were now available to help the evacuation. The weather also assisted. Low cloud combined with palls of black smoke from burning oil storage tanks blacked out the loading area to the Luftwaffe. The sea, however, was essentially calm. Nevertheless, there were sinkings and casualties arising from collisions and mines.

The 29th witnessed a superb effort to increase the pace of departure and over 47,000 were taken off: 33,558 from the mole and 13,752 from the beaches. Unfortunately, the weather improved after midday and the damage inflicted by German aircraft was extensive. Even before daylight had dawned, Wednesday the 29th had begun badly. Two destroyers, *Wakeful* and *Grafton* were both sunk in the darkness, the first by an E-boat, the second by a U-boat as she tried to rescue survivors from the first attack. The torpedo fired by *U-62* struck near to the wardroom of *Grafton*, where thirty-five rescued army officers were asleep. None survived. The captain of *Wakeful* had the misfortune to be thrown into the sea twice that night. Washed from the bridge, he was picked up by a fishing boat after *Wakeful* disintegrated. He was again washed overboard from the fishing boat but rescued by a Norwegian steamer, packed with French troops. The attempt to use the crossing over the sandbank produced damage to some ships' propellers and one destroyer temporarily grounded. But it was the Luftwaffe in the clearing skies of the afternoon that caused the most damage that day. Perhaps the worst event was the sinking of the destroyer *Grenade*, while loading at the jetty. Already full of troops she took a direct hit at four in the afternoon and exploded into flames which – luckily, only after being towed clear from the pier – blew her magazines. Hardly anyone survived. The largest ship taking part in the evacuation, the cargo steamer *Clan MacAlister* of 6,000 tons was hit by a diving Stuka while waiting off the beaches and after a second direct hit had to be abandoned. Eleven naval vessels were lost that day, including three of the precious destroyers. Some modern destroyers were in consequence withdrawn. In addition, also limiting the already impressive total of evacuees for the day, Ramsay formed the impression that the mole and outer harbour were unusable and ordered loading there abandoned. A whole night's loading was thus lost and it was only on the morning of the 30th that it was realised that the jetty could still be used.

30 May–4 June: Deliverance

Anglo-French Tensions

There was considerable tension between the two allies as the evacuation began and proceeded. At root this arose from differing perceptions of what had happened and what should happen. To Gort and many of the British, they were the victims of French incompetence. On his return, Gort roundly abused many of his ex-French colleagues: the dead General Billotte as 'completely flabby', Blanchard as 'professorial'. Sir John Dill, the new British CIGS, put it bluntly in a minute of the 29th, to Eden: 'We should say [...] that through the failure of their Army we have lost the BEF.' To the French the British appeared untrustworthy and selfish. Weygand, the new French Commander-in-Chief expressed it simply: 'Apart from his distinguished qualities, the Englishman is motivated by instinctive selfishness.' There was a widely held view that Gort had sabotaged the last hope of a counter-attack by his switch of forces to defend his northern flank. The refusal to send ever more British fighters into the battle rankled. The Dunkirk evacuation seemed to be simply a running away and leaving France to her fate.

Anglo-French Tensions

The possibilities of the future also caused tension. Churchill intended to fight on. If France were lost then Britain and her empire would continue the struggle and for this the men of the BEF were necessary. For Weygand, by this time, the best that could be hoped for was a negotiated peace. Evacuation of Dunkirk was not accepted as French policy till the 29th. Until then there was the assumption that the armed refuge would continue as a thorn in the German rear, absorbing their men and inhibiting the conquest of the rest of France. Even when the French agreed to the principle of evacuating their forces, now swelled by the III Corps of the First Army, there was the issue of priority and the shipping available, not to mention the issue of the rearguard. France was to provide 160 ships to Britain's 700. At times British sailors turned away French soldiers to fill up with their compatriots instead. Gort's line had been that 'every Frenchman embarked is at the cost of one Englishman'. Captain Tennant, on his arrival in Dunkirk, reported to the Admiralty that 'the French at Dunkirk feel strongly that they are defending Dunkirk for us, which is largely true.' This truth could be illustrated by the figures for evacuation. By the end of 30 May, only 6,000 out of the 120,000 taken to Britain so far were French.

To ease tensions, Churchill flew to Paris on the 31st and promised that withdrawal should be on equal terms, in Churchill's famous phrase, uttered in his usual execrable French accent, 'Bras dessus bras dessous.' He also promised that the British would form the rearguard. Gort was ordered to leave on the 31st but before doing so informed Admiral Abrial, the French commander in Dunkirk, that the three remaining British divisions under Alexander would be placed under French control. Contradictory signals from London to Alexander were to cause more bad feeling with a sense growing in the French High Command that Gort had lied. It was once again a case of perfidious Albion prepared to fight to the last Frenchman. To some extent French resentment was assuaged by the massive lift of French troops over the first three days in June but at least 30,000 French troops remained to be captured and had played a major part in enabling the British to escape. To these might be added the even larger number of French troops forced to surrender after being surrounded at Lille. Again their fight had increased the chances of escape for the BEF. The 'deliverance' looked very much like betrayal to many Frenchmen.

Dunkirk and the Fall of France

Defending the Perimeter

The western end of the beachhead was held by the French. Originally running from Gravelines, 10 miles from Dunkirk, inland for 6 or 7 miles and then eastwards to the old fortified town of Bergues, the French withdrew eastwards towards Dunkirk on the 27th to a new line running from Mardyck, some 5 miles from Dunkirk, inland to Spycker, and then along a canal to Bergues. The British held the line along the Bergues–Furnes Canal to Nieuport and Nieuport Bains on the coast. It was a potentially strong defensive position.

The canal was 15–20 metres wide with steep banks and much of the land around had been flooded. By the 30th most of the BEF had reached the refuge. Outside, at the edge of roads, a seemingly endless line of abandoned and wrecked lorries and other vehicles marked the end of the retreat for the BEF. The 3rd Division was one of the last to enter at Furnes with the 7th Guards leading the way. They were described as looking in good order, as if on a day's exercise at Pirbright. Montgomery, the division's commander, was as perky and bouncy as ever. They were soon under assault to the east of Furnes. German forces succeeded in crossing the canal but the newly arrived Coldstream Guards counter-attacked and drove them back, the leader of the assault, Major Campbell, suffering fatal wounds in the process. During the 31st, fierce attacks were launched all along the eastern perimeter from Furnes to Nieuport, held by the 3rd and 4th Divisions. The 2nd Grenadiers successfully counter-attacked, organised by young Second Lieutenant Jones. Three of his immediate superiors had just been killed. The German attack threatened the 4th Royal Berkshires near to Furnes and the Royal Berkshires had suffered grievously the previous day and were almost at the end of their tether. Jones's heroism restored the situation and won him the MC. Likewise, the East Surreys of the 4th Division were stretched by repeated heavy attacks around Nieuport. Unexpected assistance appeared in the form of a combined air strike by RAF Blenheims and Fleet Air Arm Albacores. The perimeter held throughout the day. Late on, the order came to pull back from the eastern end of the perimeter between Nieuport and Furnes towards the beaches, ready to embark. Most began moving at 10pm, leaving a rearguard to hold on till 2am.

The line at Bergues and immediately to the east was defended by units from the 1st Division, interspersed with units from the 42nd

(East Lancashire) Division. Six understrength battalions faced four German divisions by 1 June. This now became the main centre of the German thrust and fierce fighting ensued. The Loyal Regiment had held the town of Bergues but during the morning of the 1st, German troops managed to cross the canal to the east and establish bridgeheads. The Loyals were pulled out of Bergues and, suffering terrible casualties, counter-attacked, pushing most of the Germans back. A particularly vicious conflict erupted further to the east against the line held by the 1st East Lancs. Here the enemy was the German 20th Motorised Division. The East Lancs had repelled initial attacks on the 31st but early on the Saturday morning a massive artillery and mortar attack, lasting over two hours, indicated a new and greater assault. The crisis point of the attack, when it came, developed around an isolated barn held by a small forward detachment. Captain Harold Ervine-Andrews made his way to it with a small additional force of volunteers and finding ammunition low and the Bren jammed, deployed his skills as a marksman, picking off seventeen attackers from the blazing roof of the barn. When some Germans did manage to approach the barn they were thrown back in hand-to-hand fighting: 'When the ammo ran low, we kicked, choked, even bit them.' The Bren was repaired and after Ervine-Andrews had demonstrated his superb marksmanship yet again, the barn was held until the early evening, when, out of ammunition, the detachment withdrew. But Ervine-Andrews and the other eight unwounded soldiers let the Bren carrier go with the wounded while they themselves waded and swam their way back to the beaches, which they finally reached on the 3rd.

To their east the 2nd Coldstream fought a very effective delaying action along the canal. Some of the Bren guns' firing pins actually melted from overuse and many of their officers were killed. Among them the impressive figure of Major Angus McCorquodale, who was determined that not only his men but those of neighbouring units hold the line. He was a somewhat eccentric figure who objected to the new-style battledress, declaring: 'I don't mind dying for my country but I'm not going to die dressed like a third-rate chauffeur.' He was as good as his word, his corpse found in the resplendent old-style uniform. On their left, fierce fighting by the King's Own and the 2nd Sherwood Foresters against the German 14th Division nearly led to a German breakthrough, but it was halted at the last minute by the combined action of several units, including some of the few remaining light tanks of the Royal Inniskilling Dragoons.

As darkness fell no real breakthroughs had occurred and the Germans were as exhausted as the defenders. All of these began to pull down to the beaches and by dawn, some 6,000 remaining British troops were concentrated around the seaside resort of Malo les Bains on the eastern outskirts of Dunkirk. What was left of the perimeter was now in the hands of the French and their final heroic defence equals anything that the British had so far done.

Escape

Lieutenant-General Brooke, commander of II Corps, was ordered to return home on Thursday, 30 May, and made his usual end of the day diary entry, this time on board the destroyer HMS *Worcester*. He had handed over command of II Corps to Montgomery and in an uncharacteristic show of emotion, wept as he said farewell in the sand dunes. No man had done more to save the BEF and the strain must have been enormous and never shown, hence the surprise of Colonel Horrocks, just promoted to command a brigade of the 3rd Division and a witness to the parting scene. Brooke's entry for the 30th conveys the tension that even privileged evacuees could feel about embarkation and the crossing:

> Went down to the beach at 7.15pm, was carried out to open boat, and with Ronnie Stanyforth and Barney Charlesworth we paddled out to the destroyer and got aboard – we have been waiting till 10pm before starting, rather nerve wracking as the Germans are continually flying around and being shot at, and after seeing the ease with which a few bombs can sink a destroyer, it is an unpleasant feeling.

In fact they didn't start till 12.15 and at 3am were startled by a loud crash. Brooke was convinced they had hit a mine or been torpedoed but as he explained:

> I heard later from the commander that he had 3 routes to select from, one was under gunfire from the coast, one had had a

submarine and mines reported in it, and the other was very shallow at low water. He chose the latter and hit the bottom, damaging a propeller slightly. Finally arrived at Dover at 7.15am, wonderful feeling of peace after the last 3 weeks.

Brooke drew attention to the threat of air attack but in fact the 30th was not a favourable one for the Luftwaffe. A grey overcast sky with mist and smoke hiding the beaches was ideal. True there was more of a swell making the loading of small boats on the beaches difficult but it was not impossible. Weather was, in many ways, the decisive factor in the evacuation. It had favoured the Germans through much of the campaign: now, for much of the time, it didn't. For the British, the ideal combination was a calm sea and low cloud. Despite the swell on the 30th and some similar difficulties in the morning of the 31st, most observers remarked on the extraordinary calmness of the sea, likened to the proverbial millpond. It is worth remembering what the weather was to be like in late May and early June, four years later. Heavy seas and crashing waves nearly prevented the Allied D-Day invasion and subsequent reconquest of France. What might so easily have happened was demonstrated on 6 June 1940 when the wind got up and waves crashed into the now-deserted beaches, empty apart from the huge detritus of war. In addition, the hazard posed by clear blue skies was amply demonstrated on 29 May and 1 June. On both of these days the losses of ships inflicted by the Luftwaffe was unacceptable to the Admiralty and threatened the success of the whole operation.

Men's perceptions and experiences of these days were inevitably varied, making it dangerous to generalise about panic, chaos, Anglo-French relations, and so on. Some were very hungry. One gunner from the Royal Artillery wrote of the hunger he and his mates felt on Wednesday, the 29th, not having eaten for days. One of their number went to investigate a promising-looking van that had been abandoned. It was full of dead bodies. They eventually found some hard army biscuits. In complete contrast, downed pilot, R. A. L. Morant described a scene he witnessed at Malo les Bains on the following Saturday:

One rather amusing thing I saw was a party of French soldiers who had dug two trenches in the sands and were using the ridge between the trenches, in which they sat, as a table; over it they had a clean white tablecloth and were happily tucking in to a good meal on British rations while a bombing raid was going on about them.

Most comment on the heaps of abandoned vehicles, some used effectively to create piers into the sea, to aid the loading. There was one such at Bray Dunes, much used. Dead horses disfigured the beach and towns. The stench in Dunkirk itself from rotting horseflesh added to the sense of hell. Human corpses were plentiful, both on the beach and in the water. Many were buried, their graves marked simply by an upturned rifle. Those that were not were at least usually covered, if badly mutilated. Pilot Officer Morant commented on his surprise at how quickly the pigment of the body turned yellow. Some described the anxiety of waiting as uppermost, others lived as in a surreal dream. Some waded out in the hope of rescue, some of these being pushed out of their depth by those behind and subsequently drowned. Most, it must be remembered, were marshalled by naval ratings to the East Mole and at the appropriate time trudged along it to a waiting destroyer, or ferry. Over twice as many left from the outer harbour and its mole than left from the beaches.

The myth of the hundreds of little boats, crewed by civilian volunteers, flooding across the Channel to rescue the BEF is firmly embedded in the national psyche. In reality, most boats were crewed by the Royal Navy or the RNR or RNVR. This does not detract from those civilians who did volunteer to accompany their craft and risked their lives to save the beleaguered army. Whether crewed by service personnel or civilians it was an impressive sight from the air. Squadron Leader C. G. Lott recalled the scene on Saturday the 1st as he was flying top cover:

Big boats, little boats, boats with brass funnels, boats with strings of smaller boats strung out behind them like a duck with her ducklings. In a never-ending stream they crept over the water in both directions. The slowness of their movement was anguishing. Their vulnerability to air attack was so obvious as to make the spectacle truly heroic, and I could both have cheered and wept as I watched.

Escape

Steadily from the 30th, the BEF – and, increasingly, a large element of the French First Army – was removed. Thursday and Friday – the last two days of this momentous May – were crucial. There was a huge increase in the numbers lifted from the beaches as a result of several factors: the arrival of many more small boats, able to ferry troops out to the waiting larger ships, the creation of the piers from lorries, and the organisation of loading by Tennant and his naval teams. The lorry piers were particularly useful in speeding the process of loading the small boats, which did not now have to be run ashore and relaunched in a most tiring fashion for their naval crews. The numbers lifted from the beaches more than doubled to 29,512 on the 30th. This was to be the highest total achieved in the whole evacuation and the only day when the numbers leaving the beaches exceeded those leaving from the outer harbour. Here, although there was a late start, following the heavy damage to ships on the 29th, the fast loading of destroyers made an impact and the First Sea Lord made the brave decision to send back in the most modern destroyers of the fleet, which had been withdrawn in view of the air attacks of the previous day. However, it was two old destroyers, HMS *Wolsey* and HMS *Sabre* that achieved record totals. *Wolsey* made three trips on the 30th and lifted 1,677 men and *Sabre* packed 1,700 into two trips. The cloud cover impeded the Luftwaffe but there were still hazards from mines, E-boats and U-boats, and the sheer chaos of crowded shipping channels filled with debris and wrecks. No British destroyers were lost on either the Thursday or Friday, but a British minesweeper was bombed in one of the intermittent air raids and two French destroyers were lost – one to a mine and another to a combination of torpedoes and bombing.

Lord Gort himself left on the 31st, very unwillingly. He expressed the intention of staying with his army. The propaganda potential of his capture by the Germans was too much for Churchill, who ordered him to return when only three divisions remained. Churchill was explicit: 'No personal discretion is left to you in the matter.'

Gort initially intended to hand over to Barker, the commander of I Corps, but his nerves tested to the limit for the last two weeks were not up to it. According to Montgomery, he persuaded Gort to appoint the unflappable, aristocratic Alexander to command the beachhead on Gort's departure, stressing that Barker was not up to the job. Whether Montgomery was the decisive agent or not, Gort changed his mind and gave Alexander further chance to shine.

As the perimeter was shortened the threat from German artillery increased but despite this, Ramsay was persuaded to continue with the evacuation for another twenty-four hours, now lifting increasing numbers of French *poilus*. A heavy swell impeded beach loading on the Friday morning but conditions improved in the afternoon. Unfortunately, with better weather came the Luftwaffe, but despite some raids these were not as devastating as those on Wednesday. More and more troops were being sent along to the mole, tramping up the beaches to Dunkirk. Over 45,000 passed along the narrow wooden pier to safety this day and the combined total for Friday, despite the swell, was over 68,000. This was, of course, more in one day than had been anticipated as the total for the whole operation.

Good weather, which had returned by the evening of the 31st gave the Luftwaffe a field day on 1 June. The evacuation was now overwhelmingly from Dunkirk itself. Nieuport had been abandoned and the loading at La Panne. Some 17,348 were lifted from the remaining western end of the beaches this Saturday, compared to a staggering 47,000 from the mole. The Germans were now closing in and some German infiltrators seem to have made it into Dunkirk itself. They were brutally and effectively pushed out courtesy of a bayonet charge by several hundred guardsmen. Unfortunately, the Luftwaffe could not be so easily dealt with. Nine Stukas took on the destroyer *Basilisk* at 8.15. After repeated attacks she sank in only four fathoms of water. Many of the crew were rescued. HMS *Keith*, who had lost her previous captain in the evacuation of Boulogne also succumbed and was sunk by dive-bombers in the morning. There were further heavy raids in the early afternoon. The troop transport *Scotia* went down with the loss of 200 to 300 French soldiers, as did the minesweeper, *Brighton Queen*, loaded with Moroccan troops. Half of these were killed in the initial bombings but their discipline and good sense attracted praise and, more importantly, contributed to many being rescued. By the end of the day, thirteen British warships had been sunk as well as other vessels. It was a high price to pay, even given the large numbers rescued.

By the end of 1 June only nine of the original forty-one destroyers were undamaged. Tennant was so concerned by the end of the day, watching HMS *Worcester* creep out of the harbour, her decks awash with blood and under constant attack, that he told Alexander that daytime evacuation was over and signalled this to Ramsay. Night loading would continue and many thousands of mainly French troops were brought back. On the night of the 2nd/3rd the final component of the British rearguard, the 1st King's Shropshire Light Infantry, left and Tennant sent the signal to Ramsay at 23.30: 'BEF evacuated.'

He and Alexander then toured the coast by torpedo boat with a loudhailer, calling out for any signs of further evacuees. They then set sail for Britain. Many more French troops were lifted off from the harbour that night and again on the following night, when Admiral Abrial, the French commander-in-chief was lifted off, as was his army deputy, General Fagalde. As dawn was just beginning to break, the popular and charismatic General de la Laurencie, remaining corps commander from the First Army, stepped from the pier watched by a guard of honour who, in disciplined silence, saluted his departure. Just after this, the old destroyer *Shikari* pulled out loaded with French troops. She was the last to leave. Operation Dynamo was over. It had been a staggering success: 224,686 members of the BEF, including 13,000 wounded, had escaped. In addition 141,445 Allied troops, mainly French, had also made it to the UK.

The French Rearguard
Between 30,000 and 40,000 French soldiers did not make it. These were mainly drawn from the 12eme DIM and 68eme Infantry Division. Their heroism enabled many of their compatriots – as well as the last remnants of the BEF – to 'make it'. The Germans had had to fight every inch of the way into Dunkirk. At times the French even launched counter-attacks, taking prisoners. The last of these was launched on the morning of the 3rd, holding the attackers up for a further six hours. The 68eme in the west fought to the point when some of its units were annihilated. The Germans were nearly as exhausted as their opponents and instead of pushing rapidly into the port during the night of the 3rd/4th, rested, giving the chance for more *poilus* to escape. Only at 9am on the morning of the 4th were they able to take the city, when General Beaufrere formally surrendered. As in so many other cases, the French stubborn refusal

to surrender in and around Dunkirk is completely at odds with the widely held perception of the conduct of the French Army in the summer of 1940.

The Air War

The conflict in the skies over the evacuation area has attracted much controversy and became subject to two contradictory myths. To many of the Tommies on the beaches or slowly making their way up the East Mole, the 'Brylcreem boys' of the RAF were notable by their absence. Weary soldiers cowered in holes in the sand as German aircraft strafed the beach, or they watched in horror as Stukas peeled off from their formations into screaming bombing dives upon the loading ships. Yet in reality the RAF were there: 3,561 sorties were flown, 2,739 by fighters, and fifty-five pilots were killed and eleven wounded. Few British soldiers saw RAF fighters impeding the Luftwaffe in its declared intention to abort the escape. Too often the British fighters were high above the beaches, where they could not be recognised by the suffering British troops below, or carrying out interceptions away from sight over the sea or inland away from the Dunkirk beaches. Certainly the Luftwaffe were very conscious of the RAF presence and German forces found their attempts to prevent the evacuation bitterly contested. On the other hand, Churchill and the British authorities exaggerated the damage inflicted on the Luftwaffe for propaganda purposes, anxious to serve up a victory of some sorts. The Air Ministry claimed that the RAF had inflicted a crippling defeat on Göring's planes by destroying 390 of them. This was massively exaggerated and the real losses in the area were 132, including those lost to gunfire from the ships.

Myths abound regarding both the qualities of the aircraft involved and the training and experience of the aircrews. The German Messerschmitt Bf 109 E was an excellent fighter, superior in speed to the Hurricane but slightly inferior to the Supermarine Spitfire, but to which, taking all things into consideration, it was evenly matched. The twin-engine Messerschmitt Bf 110 C, in which Göring had great faith, lacked manoeuvrability and proved vulnerable to both British fighters. Squadron Leader J. E. McComb of 611 Squadron described a wonderful example of this on Sunday 2 June:

The Air War

I saw above me a Spitfire (it turned out to be Flight Sergeant Sadler) dive into five circling Me 110s and then get trapped in the circle. They could out-dive him but he could just turn inside them so that their shells and bullets just went under his tail. Each time they fired and missed, Sadler leaned out of his cockpit and made a vulgar gesture with two fingers.

It is often argued that the Luftwaffe enjoyed more combat experience and that their pilots thus had considerable advantage. Certainly many British pilots went into action for the first time over Dunkirk. One of the flight commanders of 611, K. M. Stoddart, had his Spitfire damaged by a 109 on Sunday, 2 June and frankly admitted the cause:

Being shot up was a case of inexperience and bad recognition. I was separated from the squadron and went to join up with a friendly looking aircraft which appeared out of nowhere and was in fact a 109! Not a very glorious first sighting of a German aircraft.

Even his squadron leader, taking part in his first combat, was surprised as J. E. McComb, quoted above recalls about 2 June:

I remember the first enemy aircraft I saw was an Me 109 which flew across my bows and I was so surprised I forgot to press the firing button.

His squadron had been ordered down to the front line in Kent on 28 May and McComb gives a wonderful illustration of what the experienced combat pilot should not do facing the enemy. Waiting for orders to take off on patrol, he drank tea and as the take-off was delayed more tea then more tea. After an uneventful patrol over the beaches in which no German planes were encountered, he led his squadron homewards, desperately worried at running out of fuel and losing the whole lot in the Channel. He recalls the consequence of too much tea before flight:

I was seized with an irresistible desire to pee. For hygienic and sartorial reasons but above all lest I be charged with wetting myself through fright, which well might have been true, I undid my Sutton Harness, then my parachute, then my overalls, then my flies. Fishing about for a bit of anatomy which on a cold morning before breakfast was not easy to find, I then let fly. Meantime my brother officers had been through several steep dives and a half roll or two.

More seriously, inexperience of real combat showed in the basic British combat tactics, using the squadron formation of four Vics, each of three planes. It was a classic case of theory at odds with practice. The two wingmen were supposed to keep a look-out but in reality just put their efforts in keeping to their station and any sudden turn was likely to lose one. Pairs were much more effective but this was contrary to the 'book'. Slowly some squadrons began to abandon the book, but only after repeated failures and losses.

On the other hand it is misleading to consider all the German pilots seasoned warriors. Clearly some had developed combat experience in Poland and some, from the famous Condor Legion, had even more from their experiences in Spain. Karl-Heinz Freisner, in his ground-breaking study of the whole 1940 campaign, points out that:

> Another cliché concerns the superiority of German pilots. On average, those pilots were considerably more poorly trained than the Allied pilots.

He puts this down to the over-rapid expansion of the Luftwaffe. Certainly the experiences of some British pilots indicate that Freisner was right. Flight Lieutenant Lane of 19 Squadron attacked a group of 110s on 1 June and was of the opinion that they were all novices who should not have been let out of flying school. Possibly the experience of the four-man crew of an Anson V, flying a patrol along the Belgian coast on Saturday morning, 1 June, is evidence in the same direction. The Anson was attacked by three Me 109s from a flight of nine. It should have been a very one-sided conflict and not in the Anson's favour. Instead, after the gunner shot down two and damaged the third, the rest of the Me 109s disappeared, leaving the Anson to complete its patrol.

Overall, the losses of both sides were very comparable. The Germans certainly received a nasty shock and did not feel that they were enjoying unchallenged control of the skies. Albert Kesselring, the commander of Air Fleet 2 of the Luftwaffe, expressed the opinion in his memoirs that:

> I pointed out to Göring that modern Spitfires had recently appeared, making our air operations difficult and costly and in the end it was the Spitfires which enabled the British and French to evacuate across the water.

Dowding and Park, running British air operations, would have been pleased with this testimonial from their opponent, and it contrasts sharply with the British Army's attitudes to them. Dowding, as head of Fighter Command, faced a terrible set of dilemmas. By 4 June, he had lost 432 modern fighters since 10 May and he felt there were barely enough left to defend the United Kingdom, his primary task. What could be spared to help save the BEF were sent into action but again there was a dilemma for Park, the section commander in Kent. To have planes over Dunkirk all the time meant sending them in penny packets and therefore facing enormous odds. To send them over in force inevitably meant gaps in the day when there would be no coverage and in those gaps the vulnerable Stukas could emerge. The RAF did what it could, and if Kesselring is to be believed, this was a substantial contribution to the evacuation.

5–24 June: The Conquest of the Third Republic

Politics and Strategy

With the fall of Dunkirk the first stage of the German plan had been triumphantly completed. 'Case Yellow', as it was officially called, had exceeded all expectations and ended within three weeks, 'an improbably short time' according to Kesselring. Hitler's doubts were replaced with euphoria. He referred to it as 'the greatest battle in world history', in his Order of the Day for 5 June. Bells were to be rung for joy throughout the German Reich for three days. Now he announced a new offensive – Case Red. This was to be the final overwhelming of France. Appropriately enough, the original mind behind the whole brilliant but risky conception, General Erich von Manstein, was now to be allowed to participate as a corps commander in the western Army Group's attack southwards.

Now there was little need for subtlety or risk-taking. The Germans enjoyed an overwhelming superiority in numbers and equipment. Two great Army Groups, totalling 104 divisions, faced the French along the line of the Somme and the Aisne. The Germans were now only 50 miles north of Paris. In the west, along the Somme, von Bock's Army Group would seek to drive south to the Seine. The steel tips of his attacks would be three reconstituted Panzer corps, each containing two Panzer divisions and a motorised division. On the extreme west, between Amiens and the sea, was Rommel's 7th, part of Hoth's Corps. The other two were placed under Kleist. The latter was relieved of his subordinate Guderian, who was promoted to command the Panzers in Rundstedt's Army Group. The tension between Guderian and Kleist had not been creative and doubtless both were glad to be rid of the other. Rundstedt's eastern force thus had two Panzer corps, each similarly composed of two Panzer divisions and a motorised division. The reorganisation of the units of the German Army in preparation for this second offensive was truly remarkable and a testament to the superb efficiency of Halder's General Staff and von Bock's and Rundstedt's Staff officers. Guderian's tanks, withdrawn from the assault on the BEF towards the end of May, had to move over 150 miles back to the east and the scene of their crucial triumph of 14 May. They were positioned just west of Sedan. Given the time necessary to accomplish this redeployment, the offensive would have a staggered start. Von Bock's group would strike on the 5th but the eastern group would begin their push on the 9th. Meanwhile, the Luftwaffe both covered the redeployment of the army and launched damaging attacks on French railways and airbases.

France's position was something of a strategic nightmare. The Dutch and Belgian divisions had totally disappeared from the equation and so, more seriously, had the bulk of the BEF. Two British divisions remained on the left of the French line, the newly formed and understrength 1st Armoured Division and the 51st Highland Division. This excellent unit had escaped the Flanders trap by being placed on the frontier with Germany, prior to the German attack of 10 May, to enhance cooperation with the French and gain front-line experience. Now it was the only fully formed and equipped British unit left in France. Two more divisions in England were being made ready to reinforce it, one of them Canadian. France herself had lost the best part of her army. Twenty-four infantry divisions had been lost, including six out of the seven that were motorised. Most of the mechanised forces had been either lost or irreparably weakened. All of the three DLMs had ceased to exist. Two out of five of the light cavalry divisions were no more and although three armoured divisions had been reconstituted from the battered remnants of the four originals they had only forty tanks each, not their original allocation of 200. By pulling more troops out of the Maginot Line Weygand had forty-three infantry divisions to hold a 225-mile front. The weakened armoured units would form a strategic reserve to counter-attack breakthroughs. Weygand attempted to develop a defence in depth rather than cling to the doctrine of the continuous front, which hitherto had served France so ill. Forces were concentrated into strongpoints, known as 'Hedgehogs'. These centres of resistance were formed around a village or some natural obstacle with old 75s dug in as tank killers. The thinking was that these would hold and break up an effective attack, allowing the 'groupements de manoeuvre' to hit those units that tried to press on round the Hedgehogs. It was a promising approach and if used earlier may very well have worked. Now, with so few units remaining, it was simply the best that could be devised.

France's problems were not simply related to lack of physical resources. There was a serious lack of clear strategic direction among her leaders. Weygand prepared to fight one last battle for the sake of honour but with little hope of ultimate success and he made no arrangements for withdrawal and retreat to secondary lines of resistance. German breakthrough would spell ultimate disaster. It would be the end. In contrast, the French Premier, Paul Reynaud, wished to continue the war by retreating to France's territories in North Africa. Here considerable resources could be mobilised from the French Empire and protected by the large French Fleet and the Royal Navy, a long war of economic attrition could be waged. There were still large numbers of aircraft unused and delivery could be taken of many more ordered from the USA. This strategy depended on preparing for the evacuation of units from the South of France and such preparations Weygand was not prepared to make. Reynaud was backed by some ministers, notably Georges Mandel, the Minister of the Interior and the newly appointed Under-Secretary of State for Defence, General Charles de Gaulle. Unfortunately, there were a growing number of influential political figures who clustered around the Deputy Premier, the 84-year-old Marshal Pétain, who thought that the time for negotiation with the Germans had come.

5–10 June: Breaking the Weygand Line

Rommel

In the west, the Germans had sensibly seized bridgeheads across the Somme, when the Panzers had rushed westwards on 19–20 May. Guderian had ordered his men across the Somme at Abbeville before turning north to the Channel ports. Other bridgeheads were established south of Amiens and south of Péronne. All French attempts to destroy these jumping-off points in late May, using the newly assembled forces south of the river, failed. As fast as the French could transfer forces from the Maginot Line to create the new 10th and 7th Armies, the slow-moving German infantry marched up behind the Panzers to hold the Panzers' gains. The presence and survival of these bridgeheads led von Bock to use his three new Panzer corps to break out. One was allotted to each bridgehead. It was assumed that what had worked in more difficult circumstances on the Meuse would work now, where no river had to be crossed in the face of hostile forces. Once again the attack would follow a massive softening up operation by the Luftwaffe. The screaming Stukas would surely intimidate the French as they had at Sedan. They didn't. The French stood and fought and the old 75s took a terrible toll of the Panzers. The new strategy seemed to be working. The French Army group commander, General Besson, sent an optimistic report in the early afternoon that the French were holding the attack and inflicting heavy casualties. Kleist's two Panzer corps made hardly any progress south of Amiens and Péronne. In the west, Rommel and Hoth's Corps became bogged down in heavy fighting in the marshes of the lower Somme at Hangest and Le Quesnoy. This appeared a return to the chopping war of attrition that had marked the First World War. Colonel General List of the Twelfth Army commented:

> The French are putting up strong opposition. No signs of demoralisation are evident anywhere. We are seeing a new French way of fighting.

Rommel

The letter of a French tank officer to his wife makes the same point and totally contradicts the received opinion of French morale and fighting spirit:

> We've taken a heck of a pasting, and there's hardly anyone left, but those still here have fantastic morale [...] we no longer think about the awful nightmare we've been through. That's typical of the French soldier, if you could only know the happiness of going into a scrap with chaps like these.

The day's fighting produced renewed confidence among both troops and politicians. It was just the psychological boost that Rundstedt had so feared in the first phase. Now it came too late. No amount of raised morale could counter the material shortages of the French Army.

On the 6th, the Péronne and Amiens bridgeheads continued to be contained and in three days the 10th Panzer Division lost two-thirds of its tanks in trying to break out south of Amiens, but once again it was Rommel who achieved breakout. After fierce fighting he reached 20 miles south of the Somme, cutting off the British 51st Division and a French unit from the rest of Altmeyer's Tenth Army. On the eastern flank, along the infamous Chemin Des Dames – scene of so much fighting in 1914–1918 – the German infantry of their Ninth Army pushed the French back to the south side of the Aisne. On the 7th Rommel pushed on another 17 miles to Forges-les-Eaux. He had simply decided to ignore the 'Hedgehogs' and sweep round them across country. These were the stormtrooper tactics of 1918 applied to tank warfare. He was 25 miles from Rouen. Attempts at counter-attack failed – the French mobile reserves were too weak. The next day Rommel pressed on to Elboeuf on the Seine. The other Panzer division of Hoth's Corps, the 5th, made for Rouen, which it captured. Manstein's infantry corps had pressed on rapidly behind the tanks to increase the width of the breakthrough and reached the Seine by the 10th. Weygand recognised by the 8th that this second, less well-known Battle of the Somme was lost. Both flanks had been turned and he ordered a withdrawal. The Germans, anxious to exploit success, transferred Kleist's battered corps eastwards to exploit the breakthrough on the Aisne. Once again German staffwork showed flexibility and skill.

Guderian

At 5am the eastern half of the battle began, but because there were no convenient bridgeheads as jumping-off points, Rundstedt ordered his infantry to cross the river first, to prepare the way for Guderian's Panzers. As on the Somme, the French fought heroically. General Lattre de Tassigny, in command of the formidable 14th Division, threw the Germans back south of Rethel and took 800 prisoners. Guderian found himself unable to move and was embarrassed by a visit by his superior, General List, who found the Panzer troops relaxing – and even some bathing in a nearby stream – while waiting for the chance to move. Uncharacteristically immobile, Hurrying Heinz had to explain that it was not his task to establish a bridgehead. A small bridgehead had actually been established at Château Porcien to the west of Rethel, and under cover of darkness Guderian decided to pass the 1st Panzer Division across and then the 2nd. The result was a breakthrough to the south and on the 10th a hard-fought tank battle with elements of the remaining French mobile reserve. The quality of the French tanks was clear from Guderian's description of the battle, but the French 3rd Armoured had few left:

> A tank battle developed to the south of Juniville, which lasted for some two hours before being eventually decided in our favour. In the course of the afternoon Juniville itself was taken. There Balck managed personally to capture the colours of a French regiment [...] While the battle was in progress I attempted, in vain, to destroy a Char B with a captured 47mm anti-tank gun; all the shells I fired at it simply bounced harmlessly off its thick armour. Our 37mm and 20mm guns were equally ineffective against this adversary. As a result, we inevitably suffered sadly heavy casualties.

The German infantry, with heavy artillery support, ground down the French 'Hedgehogs' and with too few mobile forces to counter the Panzers, the front was broken. Despite local successes the French tanks were simply too few to turn the scale of the battle. Heinz could once again hurry, rushing almost unopposed through the French countryside. The 2nd Panzer Division reached the outskirts of

11–14 June: The Briare Conference and the Fall of Paris

Rheims on the 10th. Now Kleist's reallocated Panzers could join the chase, pushing down to the Marne, east of Paris.

By the evening of the 10th, the Germans were to the west of Paris on the lower Seine and to the east of the capital on the Marne. The French Government decided to abandon Paris for Tours on the Loire. This was devastating. In 1914, as the Germans reached the Marne and threatened Paris, the French had counter-attacked and saved France. There could be no counter-attack this time. The French writer, André Maurois, wrote of the significance of the decision:

> At that moment I knew everything was over. France deprived of Paris, would become a body without a head. The war had been lost.

That same day Italy declared war. France would now face over thirty Italian divisions on her south-eastern frontier.

11–14 June: The Briare Conference and the Fall of Paris

Military Headquarters had been pulled back to the town of Briare on the Upper Loire on 9 June. This, it was hoped, was sufficiently far south to be safe from marauding Panzers. The building contained a single telephone and, totally dependent on the local exchange, was non-operative for one hour in the middle of the day while the lady operator took her lunch. It was to this auspicious venue that the great and the good of the Allies repaired on the 11th, for a major review of strategy. Monsieur Reynaud, the French Premier, was accompanied by Marshal Pétain, his deputy, General Weygand and the recently appointed de Gaulle. Churchill arrived with the Foreign Secretary, Anthony Eden, General Ismay, Secretary of the War Cabinet and General Spears, Liaison Officer with the French Government. The conference began at 7pm with a lengthy and wholly pessimistic report from Weygand. Churchill urged a street-by-street defence of Paris to sap the strength of the Germans. Pétain made it quite clear that this was not going to happen. The French capital would not be reduced to rubble to hold up the Germans for a few days. There were repeated demands on Churchill for more air support, which he consistently refused. Weygand stressed that now was the decisive moment. Churchill, already anticipating what was to come, argued that it would be when the Luftwaffe was thrown against Britain. Weygand mentioned that France might have to ask for an armistice and the divisions in the French leadership were exposed when Reynaud snapped that this was a political matter. Despite Reynaud's hostility, he was under real pressure from Pétain to seek peace, as he later told Churchill. With nothing settled, the British Prime Minister and his entourage left after a brief meeting the following morning. He had arrived with an escort of twelve Hurricanes but cloud prevented their presence for the return. Assured that it was likely to be cloudy all the way to London, Churchill decided to return without escort. The history of the twentieth century could have been very different if two Luftwaffe pilots had been more alert. The cloud cleared as Churchill's plane reached the coast. Two German pilots were too busy firing at fishing boats to see the flamingo transport and its precious cargo. Churchill reached Hendon Airport unscathed. Would Britain have continued fighting without him? The risk of such flights had no deterrent effect and he returned the next day for further talks with Reynaud at Tours. Little was accomplished: it would be four years before Churchill set foot in France again.

On the day that Churchill arrived at Briare to plead for a bitter defence of Paris, the French Government declared it an open city and by the 13th the last French troops had left. German forces were already close to the outskirts. Next morning a lieutenant-colonel, Dr Hans Speidel, took the surrender of the city and German infantry of the 87th Division moved in peacefully. Rifles and Spandau machine guns were quickly put aside for cameras. The warriors were transformed into tourists.

To the west of Paris, Rommel continued to garner more military laurels. His forces swung north-west from the Seine towards the isolated elements of the Tenth Army in and around St Valery-en-Caux on the coast. The cut-off British and French forces had retreated there in the hope of evacuation. The site was unsuitable and following the orders of his superior French corps commander, General Fortune felt obliged to surrender himself and the whole of his 51st Highland Division to captivity on 12 June. To the east of Paris, Guderian's Panzers reached Chalons sur Marne by the 12th. His advance south-eastwards threatened to cut off the vast numbers of French troops on the frontier and manning the Maginot Line. The French commander, General Pretelat, had already made two requests to Weygand for permission to make plans for withdrawal. Weygand refused until the 12th. It was too late and Pretelat only began the essential strategic retreat on the 14th. By this time Guderian's forces had rushed towards the south and east, cutting off any such retreat. Guderian, in his memoirs, paints a picture of a headlong dash, with infantry units jostling Panzers to get at the enemy and press further into France. Once again the indestructible Balck makes an appearance. Guderian came upon him by the Rhine–Marne Canal. Asked if he had secured a bridgehead, Balck rather hesitatingly agreed that he had. Guderian discovered that in so doing Balck had disobeyed corps' orders to halt at the canal. Here, again, is an illustration of the aggressive initiative shown by relatively junior officers in thrusting forward. Early on the 14th the 1st Panzer Division had reached St Dizier, taking considerable prisoners from the French 3rd Armoured, the 3rd North African and the 6th Colonial Divisions. In Guderian's words: 'they gave the impression of being utterly exhausted.' By the early morning of the 15th, Langres had fallen with yet more prisoners. But even more disastrously for France, a further 400,000 French soldiers were now trapped in a vast pocket between Nancy and Belfort.

15–24 June: Endgame and Armistice

By the 15th, the campaign was effectively decided. In the west Rommel was to set a new record for a daily advance. He covered 150 miles on 17 June and on the 19th took Cherbourg. During Case Red, as during Case Yellow, the achievements of his 7th Panzer Division had been remarkable, capturing 97,648 prisoners for the loss of 682 killed. In the same period, Guderian's forces swept on to the Swiss frontier at Pontarlier by the 17th, and then swung north to the Maginot Line. It was clearly over for the French Army, which secured an armistice with Germany on the 22nd.

The final defeat of France involved a second British evacuation from France, south of the Somme. There were considerable numbers of British forces, both fighting units – like the 1st Armoured Division – and line of communication troops. Churchill initially hoped to build up a new BEF of four divisions, using the Canadians and the 52nd Lowland Division. There were dreams, even as the scale of the

French collapse became apparent, of creating a stronghold or redoubt in Brittany, from which the Germans could be defied. To command this new BEF, Brooke was sent back, strongly suspecting that the whole episode was a futile gesture. Knighted at Buckingham Palace on the 11th, he was in Cherbourg by the evening of the 12th, the day that one of his divisions, the 51st Highland, had been forced to surrender to Rommel on the Normandy coast. Brooke went to see both Weygand and Georges and their attitudes confirmed his sense of futility. They made it clear there were not enough troops to establish a defensive perimeter in Brittany. On the 14th he decided British troops should be withdrawn – the newly arrived Canadians to leave from Brest and the 52nd to retire to Cherbourg. Others were dispatched to Nantes for embarkation. Brooke had a difficult time convincing Churchill when a telephone link was established with 10 Downing Street, and he was heard to say: 'You've lost one Scottish Division. Do you want to lose another?' In his diary he confesses to being repeatedly on the verge of losing his temper. Churchill told him that he had been sent to make the French feel that Britain was supporting them: 'I replied that it was impossible to make a corpse feel.' In the end Churchill agreed.

Brooke succeeded in evacuating the vast bulk of British forces still in France. A total of 144,171 British troops were taken off, in addition to several thousand allies, including nearly 25,000 Polish troops. In addition, 300 guns were successfully withdrawn for future use. Nearly 60,000 left from Nantes/St Nazaire, which was to be the scene of the outstanding disaster of this second and little-known withdrawal. Here the liner *Lancastria* was hit by bombs on the afternoon of the 17th. Although nearly 2,500 were rescued over 3,000 were drowned. It was so disastrous, news was kept from the public. Brooke himself left St Nazaire next day on a trawler, reaching Plymouth on the 19th. He had been right about the French inability to continue the struggle.

Reynaud had lost the political struggle with Pétain and on the 16th resigned. Churchill had offered an indissoluble union of the two countries but the French Cabinet rejected it out of hand. Pétain likened it to union with a corpse – coming from the octogenarian marshal, who was himself described as a wheezing skeleton, this was possibly a simile too far. Weygand, Pétain and a majority of the

15–24 June: Endgame and Armistice

leading figures in the Third Republic, felt that Britain was finished and the thought of abandoning metropolitan France to continue the war in North Africa quite unacceptable. As one of them said, France would become another British Dominion. Not all agreed and Brigadier de Gaulle took off for London in the plane carrying Sir Edward Spears home, his liaison mission over. However, to most of France's military and political leaders, it seemed better to seek accommodation with the new ruler of Europe. Pétain replaced Reynaud and the next day sought an armistice through the good offices of Spain. On the same day, the 17th, he broadcast to the French people that the fighting must stop, and the words of the old relic of World War One sapped the will to resist in many units – but not all. The officer cadets at Saumer held the bridges over the Loire for two days till their ammunition ran out.

Italy had thirty-two divisions on the Alpine Front. Mussolini had delayed his declaration of war till it appeared that France was defeated and to delay longer risked exclusion from potential spoils. Facing the Italians was a small French force of three B class divisions, like those that had received the brunt of the German attacks at Sedan, plus three fortress divisions. This tiny Army of the Alps was thus outnumbered five-to-one. It had, however, the advantage of the rugged Alpine terrain and a competent commander, General Olry, who had prepared his positions well, with carefully chosen positions for his artillery and excellent observation posts. In addition, plans had been prepared to block the narrow Alpine passes, massively increasing the Italian logistic problems. The Italians may have declared war on the 10th but there was no offensive activity until the 20th, when the Germans had reached the Rhône Valley and threatened Olry's force from the rear. The attacks on the Mont Genevre Pass were blocked, as were almost all others. Despite small successes, on the 21st and 22nd, when the armistice came into force on the 24th, the French had barred the Italian advance from Switzerland to the coast. French B divisions, when well lead and prepared, could fight well and effectively.

Aftermath

Conclusions

The sheer rapidity and apparent one-sidedness of the German victory have led successive analysts to see France's defeat as inevitable, the consequence of deep-seated causes, social, economic, political and military. There is a natural tendency to believe that great events have great causes. Historians are programmed to be multicausal, and the more profound, the more intellectually satisfying the analysis becomes. It is always possible to discover social fractures and weaknesses in political structures, which can be used to demonstrate why some event was likely. France certainly had her share of bitter political divisions in the 1930s and the legacy of the First World War had undoubtedly strengthened anti-militarism in France, Britain and Belgium – but so it had in many segments of German society. Hitler was deeply disappointed in the apathy of German people towards war: 'What am I to do with these people?' he is reported as saying, following the poor and glum response of the Berlin crowds to a military parade in 1938. Had Germany failed in 1940 – and it needs restating that most of the German military expected it to fail – then numerous learned articles could have been written on the structural weaknesses of the German war economy, the increasing need of the Nazi regime to resort to repression and the divisions both within the ruling party and between the party and the army. In the end the miraculous victory of this summer of 1940 swept away doubts about the Nazi regime and consolidated Hitler's power. The contention here is that this was not inevitable but a mixture of certain key German advantages and French mistakes – plus a good dose of luck.

France suffered from some deep-seated disadvantages vis-à-vis Germany. Demographically she could not match her eastern neighbour and the number of young men available for call-up in 1939 was half those available to Germany. The 1930s had been marked by bitter clashes between extreme right and extreme left.

Then, as now, France has a far bigger percentage of its population prepared to vote for the revolutionary left and/or the semi-fascist right, than is the norm in Britain. In 1939–1940 this had some impact. Some young militant Communists did try to sabotage war production, dropping handfuls of screws and bolts into the gears of new French tanks or weakening the fuel pipes of aircraft. Some on the right feared revolution more than the Germans and by mid June this came to the fore in people like Pétain. Possibly as a result of opposition to war, for whatever reason, some French units were less than enthusiastic about fighting and broke early when under attack. The French command structure was rigid and over complex. Gamelin relied on personal contact rather than the telephone or radio from his headquarters at Vincennes. The belief in the methodical battle had a somewhat stultifying effect on initiative and contributed to the slow response at times of crisis. Many French fighters were obsolete and the mission rate per day was far below that of the Luftwaffe or even the RAF. There was a shortage of anti-tank guns and mines and some French tanks were without radios. Considering all the above, defeat might appear inevitable.

However, on the other side of the ledger, the building of the Maginot Line was a far-sighted and effective response to France's demographic difficulties and given time, Britain, with France would outnumber Germany. For all the ideological divisions in France, there was an overwhelming unity in the face of the enemy. Outbreaks of sabotage were trivial compared to the massive surge in war production that continued from 1939 into May 1940. Tanks, modern aircraft, anti-tank guns, were being produced as never before and were ready for distribution to the front. French troops fought with determination and bravery, with the exception of the crucial units at Sedan and in the period of disorientation immediately after the German breakthrough. The best German units had struck the weakest French units. But where the Panzers struck the first-class units of the French First Army, as at Gembloux, the French held. All armies can become subject to panic as a result of unexpected and difficult circumstances, hence the disintegration of the Ninth Army following the Meuse breakout. German units panicked at various times, as at Arras. The gloom of defeat or the exhilaration of victory was all-important to morale and future performance. The experienced commander of Army Group A, von Rundstedt, was well aware of this from his experiences of 1914 and was anxious for the French not to be given the morale-boost of a small victory. But when small victories did come, it was too late to alter the bigger strategic situation. French command and control was over rigid but the overall strategy was fundamentally right and was the one that eventually led to the defeat of Nazi Germany. Sheer weight of resources would eventually tell. France was planning on a long war. Aircraft were held deliberately back to ensure replacements were available as a result of the attrition of battle. Even the oft quoted mistake by Gamelin of not embracing radio communication at Vincennes arose not from stupidity or a distrust and ignorance of new technology, but an appreciation of its insecurity given the potential of code-breaking – an area in which the French were ahead of the Germans. In this they looked forward to the enormous contribution made to the Allied victory at Bletchley Park. Their mistake was to exaggerate in 1940 the capacity to break codes quickly, so as to be tactically effective. In other ways France was ahead of her rival. French equipment was, in many ways, superior, and the French Army in many ways more modern. French troops had more motor transport; their tanks were superior in weight of armour and firepower; and in sheer numbers of artillery, the French massively outclassed the Germans. There were, in short, many reasons for senior German officers to be pessimistic about their chances of success on 10 May.

The senior German commanders were very conscious of their deficiencies. The German Army had only half the artillery of the combined Allied armies. Some 135 divisions faced 151 Allied divisions and forty-three of the German divisions were reserve formations with limited training and poor equipment. The French had 300,000 vehicles, the Germans only 120,000 trucks. Most of the German Army was an antique, horse-reliant force. Vehicle production in Germany was so low that it could not keep up with wear and tear, let alone equip new motorised divisions. As quoted in the introduction, Halder was seriously contemplating having to break up one of the existing ones. Fuel supplies were very problematic. Only sixteen divisions were 'modern', i.e. ten Panzer divisions and six motorised divisions. Even here, most of the German tanks were obsolete and inferior in firepower and armour to the

French. As pointed out frequently in the text above, German shells bounced off the French Char B2s and the even thicker armour of the British Matildas. The German supremacy in the air was not completely obvious before May. French production was increasing rapidly and large orders had been placed in the USA, which were being delivered during the summer. At the front Germany did achieve superiority in numbers but partly because the French chose not to deploy large quantities of aircraft, retaining them in rear areas for future use. French pilots displayed skills, probably, on balance, superior to those of the Luftwaffe, many of whom were hastily trained and highly vulnerable. Some 1,236 German planes were destroyed and 323 damaged compared to 892 French planes lost. In addition the 1,029 planes lost by the RAF need to be taken into account. By May British and French air production massively exceeded that of Germany. The attack that began on 10 May was clearly a gamble. Hitler was going for broke.

The gamble paid off: why? First, the Germans did the unexpected, attacking through the Ardennes, which the French regarded as too risky – as did many Germans. The point of attack was almost forced on them by the loss of the original plan in January. The result was that the best German units struck the weakest French and shattered the front. The impact of surprise was made all the greater by the uncharacteristically risky strategy of Gamelin, who sent his reserve army, the Seventh under Giraud, north to the Dutch frontier. This so-called 'Breda variation' of the French advance into Belgium was a dream scenario for the German planners. The speed then of the advance from the Meuse after the 14th destabilised the French, who responded too slowly. Panic and fear became key allies to the rampaging Panzers. The Germans had stumbled into Blitzkrieg almost by accident, as the hesitancy and nerves of Kleist, von Rundstedt and Hitler indicate. Undoubtedly the air support of the Luftwaffe contributed, and the closer cooperation of land forces and air power on the Germans' part – compared to that of the Allies – was a marked advantage, possibly a decisive one in the crossing of the Meuse at Sedan. Throughout the campaign as a whole, the Luftwaffe threw everything into the assault rather than preparing for a long struggle, for which they lacked the spares and ammunition. They, too, like Hitler, were going for broke. There can be little doubt that the training and tactical doctrines of the German Army in its armoured spearhead and first wave infantry divisions was superb. As Brooke pointed out in his diary entry for 23 May: 'There is no doubt that they are most wonderful soldiers.'

Initiative was encouraged at a junior level and on many occasions the heroic acts of individuals mattered: Sergeant Rubarth, crossing the Meuse at Sedan; Rommel securing a passage further north and later blazing off into the blue out of contact with Corps HQ. No individual symbolises this more than Lieutenant Colonel Hermann Balck, the 'Richard Sharpe' of the German Army. By comparison, French tactical training stressed methodical obedience to received orders. They saw logic and planning as the keys to victory. The Germans embraced chaos, recognising the anarchy of the battlefield and the need for rapid pragmatic response. The German Army and Air Force also enjoyed the inestimable advantage of practice, notably in Poland. The French were having to learn many of the lessons that the Germans had acquired. This was particularly true for the newly established French armoured divisions.

In addition, there was a large element of luck. The Germans consistently threw sixes. The weather was superb for tanks and aircraft. The effects of rain on the 28th indicate what might have happened, had the weather broken earlier. The Belgian *chasseurs* withdrew too soon from the Ardennes. Guderian was lucky in escaping death at Semois, as was Rommel on several occasions. Bilotte, by comparison, was killed in a car accident. Guderian was again lucky at Sedan, in the failure of Kleist's altered orders for bombing patterns to reach the Luftwaffe in time. He certainly regarded his continuous bombing pattern, which was stuck to – despite Kleist's disagreement – as vital to the success of the crossing. Further north, where Rommel crossed the Meuse, the weir was underguarded because of the unfortunate death of the responsible French officer. Even so, the Meuse crossings nearly failed. Only three of the six succeeded and it was touch-and-go.

Once again, luck was to be a decisive factor in the Dunkirk operation: this time the British were able to throw sixes. The unusually calm seas facilitated the evacuation. The cloud cover on several days, particularly the 28th and the 30th, reduced the threat from the Luftwaffe. The German halt order on the 24th was almost the miracle that Brooke had stated as being necessary in his diary entry for the 23rd. However, in addition to luck, there were a host of human virtues: the professionalism of the Royal Navy under the leadership of Ramsay and Tennant, the planning of Adam and Lawson in laying out the perimeter, the superb staffwork of Brooke, the contribution of the RAF and, above all, the heroism and dogged determination of most of the British troops.

The reputation of the British Field Force has of course suffered, for although Dunkirk may have been a deliverance – partially mitigating for the British the humiliation of a lost campaign – it still was a lost campaign. The loss of heavy equipment and transport was on a colossal scale. For the army that had played such a significant part in the defeat of Germany in 1918, it was a humiliating reversal of roles. The result has been a self-flagellating campaign to find explanations. It is widely believed that the BEF was poorly equipped. The film *Dunkirk*, made in 1958, has one of the characters alluding to the need to fight the Germans with our bare hands. Montgomery, in an oft quoted passage from his memoirs, referred to the poor quality of much of the transport. Soldiers at the time, and writers subsequently, have drawn attention to the inadequacy of the anti-tank rifle and the shortages of anti-tank guns. The lightly armoured British Cruiser tanks and the limited firepower of the Matilda Is have likewise been advanced as instances of an underfunded and under-prepared force. Yet, similar complaints were being made in the German Army with an even greater basis in fact. The muzzle velocity of British tank guns was greater than that of German tanks, and the armour of the Matildas more than twice as thick as that of the best protected PzKpfw IIIs and IVs. The new 25-pounder and the Bren were excellent. The BEF was unique in being completely motorised and in this, a generation ahead of the bulk of the Wehrmacht. If there were faults with many of the vehicles, exactly the same was true of those minority of German units equipped with motor transport. Perhaps the last word on equipment should be left to von Bock, who, commenting on the heaps of material abandoned by the BEF, claimed that the British were equipped to a standard that the German Army could only dream of.

The BEF was defeated in France not because of its own demerits or lack of equipment but because the French High Command made key mistakes, which were ruthlessly exploited by the German front-line forces. By the third week in May the Field Force was in a strategically hopeless position through no fault of its own. Both before this, and afterwards, it performed creditably against German forces and this credit is seldom acknowledged. In holding the line south of Ypres on 25–28 May, a crucial defensive battle was won. Various other small-scale defensive actions like those at Boulogne, Calais, Cassel or on the perimeter of Dunkirk, displayed a skill and heroism too often ignored. Brooke, Montgomery and Alexander established well-deserved reputations for military competence. The fundamental problems arose from dependence on allies, over whose decisions the British had no control.

In 1940 the German Army won its greatest victory of the Second World War. It consolidated the hold of the Nazis on power within Germany and concealed the fundamental flaws in the German war economy. The victory was not inevitable. A mixture of luck, skill and mistakes by the French High Command enabled the brittle lance, that was Army Group A, to penetrate far into France and cut off the best Allied units to the north. Hitler had gone for broke and the gamble seemed to have paid off – or it had nearly paid off. The escape of the BEF was a strategic disaster for Germany, ensuring that an operational triumph would evolve into strategic defeat. The long war that both the British and French had prepared for, would continue, but without the French. Millions would die but the Third Reich would be ground into dust. Hitler really had gone for broke.

Appendix I
Biographical Notes

Belgium
Leopold III, King of the Belgians and commander-in-chief.
Michiels, Oscar, General Chief of the general staff.
Overstraeten, Raoul Van, Aide-de-camp to the king and military adviser.

France
Abrial, Jean, Admiral, commanding officer of Naval forces in the north and the garrisons of the Channel ports.
Astierde la Vigerie, François, General, commander of Allied air forces in the Northern Zone.
Billotte, Gaston Henri, General, commander of Allied forces in the north, French First, Seventh, Ninth and Second, plus BEF and Belgians.
Blanchard, Georges Marie Jean, General, commander of French First Army and then successor to Billotte.
Corap, André, General, commander of Ninth Army, north of Sedan.
Fagalde, Robert, General, commander of XVI Corps and appointed commander of land forces and the garrisons of the Channel ports under Abrial.
Gamelin, Maurice, General, supreme commander Allied Forces and French chief of staff until 19 May.
Gaulle, Charles de, Brigadier, commander French 4th Armoured Division and then under secretary at the War Ministry.
Georges, Alphonse Joseph, General, commander of the Northern Front, immediately below Gamelin.
Giraud, Henri, General, commander of Seventh and later Ninth Army.
Huntzinger, Charles, General, commander of French Second Army south of Sedan.

Mandel, Georges, Minister of the Interior and a keen opponent of an armistice.

Pétain, Henri Philippe, Marshal of France, commander of the French armies in 1917–1918 and successor to Reynaud as head of the War Cabinet on 16 June. Chief of State 1940–1944.

Pretelat, André Gaston, General, commanding officer of the Second Army Group on the eastern frontier of France.

Prioux, Rene-Jacques Adolphe, General, commander of cavalry corps in the north and finally commander of First Army in succession to Blanchard.

Reynaud, Paul, French Prime Minister to 16 June.

Weygand, Maxime, General, successor to Gamelin as supreme Allied commander 19 May.

Germany

Balck, Hermann, Lieutenant-Colonel, 1st Rifle Regiment of 1st Panzer Division.

Bock, Fedor von, General, commander of Army Group B, providing the 'matador's cloak' by invading Holland and Belgium.

Göring, Hermann, Field Marshal, commander of the Luftwaffe.

Guderian, Heinz, General, commander of XIX Panzer Corps and tank theorist who evolved Blitzkrieg in May 1940.

Halder, Franz, General, chief of the general staff.

Hitler, Adolf, Reich Chancellor and Führer, supreme commander of the Wehrmacht.

Höpner, Erich, General, commander of XVI Panzer Corps in von Bock's Army Group.

Hoth, Hermann, General, commander of XV Panzer Corps and Rommel's immediate superior.

Keitel, Wilhelm, General, chief of the Wehrmacht High Command.

Kesselring, Albert, General, commander of the 2nd Air Fleet.

Kleist, Ewald von, General, commander of Panzer Group. Guderian's immediate superior during Case Yellow.

Leeb, Wilhelm Ritter von, General, commander of Army Group C, facing the Maginot Line.

List, Wilhelm, General, commander of Twelfth Army under Rundstedt.

Manstein, Erich von, General, initially chief of staff to von Rundstedt and credited with the concept of Case Yellow. Later infantry corps commander in June.

Reinhardt, Hans, General, commander of Panzer Corps XLI.

Rommel, Erwin, General, commander of the 7th Panzer Division. Secured crucial Meuse crossing in Belgium and contributed to the evolution of Blitzkrieg.

Rubarth, Walter, Feldwebel, platoon leader 2nd Company 49th Panzer Engineer Battalion – crucial in securing Meuse crossing at Sedan.

Rundstedt, Gerd von, General, commander of Army Group A, directing the central thrust across the Meuse.

Student, Kurt, General, commander of 7th Air Division, vital in the seizure of Holland.

Netherlands

Winkelman, Henri, General, commander-in-chief of Armed Forces.

United Kingdom

Adam, Ronald, Lieutenant-General, commander of III Corps of the Field Force and then in charge of establishing the Dunkirk perimeter.

Alexander, Harold, Major-General, commander of 1st Division and of the rearguard at Dunkirk.

Barker, Michael, Lieutenant-General, commander of I Corps of the Field Force.

Barratt, Arthur, Air Marshal, commander of the RAF in France.

Brooke, Alan Francis, Lieutenant-General, commander of II Corps of the Field Force and later commander of British troops south of the Somme 12–19 June. His diary remains a valuable source.

Churchill, Winston Spencer, Prime Minister from 10 May.

Colville, John, Churchill's private secretary and author of *Downing Street Diaries*.

Dowding, Hugh, Air Chief Marshal, commanding officer of Fighter Command.

Eden, Anthony, Secretary of State for War in the Churchill Cabinet formed in May.

Franklyn, Harold E., Major-General, commander of 5th Division.

Gort, John Standish, 6th Viscount, General, commander of the Field Force.

Ironside, Edmund, General, chief of the Imperial General Staff.

Montgomery, Bernard, Major-General, commander of 3rd Division.

Pownall, Henry, Lieutenant-General, chief of staff of the Field Force.

Spears, Edward, Major-General, Churchill's liaison officer with the French Government.

Appendix II
Glossary of Terms

Army: Large body of men, usually under a full general (colonel general in the German Army), composed of several divisions organised into two or more army corps. The whole BEF constituted one army in 1940. In 1918 the BEF was composed of five armies.

Army Corps: Subdivision of an army originating in the Napoleonic Wars, only adopted by Britain in the twentieth century. An army corps would normally be commanded by a lieutenant-general and be composed of two or more divisions. The corps would provide heavy artillery support and additional specialist services. The BEF was organised into three army corps before Dunkirk. Brooke's II Corps became the biggest with four divisions by the third week in May.

Army Group: A collection of armies grouped under one commander and HQ staff. The creation of this organisation was a reflection of the growing size of military forces in the twentieth century. The BEF in 1918 was, in effect, an army group but the British forces in France were not big enough to form one in 1940 when the Field Force was part of a group under the French General Billotte. Normally commanded by either a full general or field marshal.

Battalion: Basic unit of most armies, of just under 1,000 men, but in some circumstances could be considerably smaller, as was the Territorial battalion, Queen Victoria Rifles at Calais. In the British Army usually commanded by a lieutenant-colonel but in the German, a major. Most battalions were 'brigaded' into larger units but some could be attached to GHQ or a corps as a reserve. The 1st Battalion Welsh Guards was directly attached to GHQ, whereas the 2nd was brigaded with the 2nd Irish Guards into 20 Brigade for the defence of Boulogne. British battalions were designated by their regiment, of which there could be several battalions, the lower numbers being regulars and the higher Territorial. Six battalions of the Durham Light Infantry were serving within the BEF, the 2nd in the 2nd Division, the 10th and 11th in the 23rd Division and the 6th, 8th and 9th, forming 151 Brigade of the 50th Division.

Brigade: Usually composed of three battalions in 1940 under a brigadier general. In 1918, brigades usually had four battalions. In 1940 they usually joined with two other brigades to form a division but could act independently, as at Calais or Boulogne.

Company: Subdivision of a battalion in which there were usually four, under either a captain or a major in the British Army.

Division: Basic unit of tactical command, i.e. the smallest self-sufficient unit, a miniature army. Normally composed of three brigades plus artillery and engineers and under the command of a major-general in the British Army. A division in 1940 would normally amount to 14,000 men. The 5th Division had only two brigades, one having been detached, and was consequently smaller. Sometimes divisions were designated not only by number but by the region from which most of the component battalions came: for example, the 51st Highland Division.

Platoon: Subdivision of a company, of around fifty men under either a lieutenant or second lieutenant.

Regiment: In the French and German Armies, the organisational equivalent to a British brigade, composed of three battalions. In the British Army regiments were the focus of historical and regional loyalty and the way of designating different battalions.

Section: This was the smallest unit of up to twelve men under a corporal.

Bibliography

Atkin, R., *Pillar of Fire, Dunkirk 1940*, Sidgwick & Jackson, 1990

Barnett, C. (editor), *Hitler's Generals*, W & N, 1989

Beaufre, A., *1940 the Fall of France*, Cassell (English edition), 1967

Below, N. von, *At Hitler's Side: The Memoirs of Hitler's Luftwaffe Adjutant 1937–1945*, (English edition), Greenhill Books, 2001

Black, J., *Warfare in the Western World 1882–1975*, Acumen, 2002

Blatt, J. (editor), *French Defeat of 1940: Reassessments*, Berghahn, 1998

Bond, B. and Taylor, M., *Battle For France and Flanders Sixty Years On*, Leo Cooper, 2001

Bond, B. (editor), *Diaries of Lieutenant General Sir Henry Pownall*, Volume I, 'Chief of Staff', Leo Cooper, 1972

Boyce, R. and Maiolo, J. A. (editors), *Origins of World War Two: The Debate Continues*, Palgrave Macmillan, 2003

Caffery, K., *Combat Report – The RAF and The Fall of France*, Crowood Press, 1990

Churchill, W. S. C., *Second World War*, Vol. 2, Cassell, 1949

Colville, J., *Fringes of Power: Downing Street Diaries 1939–1955*, revised edition, W & N, 2004

Cooksey, J., Boulogne *20 Guards Brigade's Fighting Defence – May 1940*, Leo Cooper, 2002

Cowley, R. (editor), *No End Save Victory*, Cassell, 2002

Cull, B., Lander, B. and Weiss, H., *Twelve Days in May – The Air Battles for Northern France and the Low Countries, May 1940*, Grub Street, 1995

Danchev, A. and Todman, D. (editors), *War Diaries of Field Marshal Lord Alanbrooke*, W & N, 2001

Dear, I. C. B. (editor), *The Oxford Companion to World War II*, OUP, 1995

Deighton, L., *Blitzkrieg*, Jonathan Cape, 1979

Dinardo, R. L., *Mechanised Juggernaut or Military Anachronism? Horses and the German Army of World War II*, Greenwood, 1991

Doughty, R. A., *Breaking Point: Sedan and the Fall of France*, Archon, 1990

Ellis, L. F., *War in France and Flanders 1939–1940*, HMSO, 1954

Evans, M. M., *Fall of France: Act with Daring*, Osprey, 2000

Franks, N., *Air Battle for Dunkirk 26 May–3 June 1940*, first published 1983, Grub Street edition, 2006

Fraser, D., *And We Shall Shock Them: The British Army in the Second World War*, Hodder and Stoughton, 1983

Fraser, D., *Alanbrooke*, HarperCollins, 1982

Freiser, K. H., *Blitzkrieg Legend* (First published in German 1996), English translation with J. T. Greenwood Naval Institute Press, 2005

Gordan, B. H. (editor), *Historical Dictionary of World War II France*, Greenwood Press, 1998

Guderian, H., *Actung – Panzer!*, first published in German 1937, English translation by C. Duffy, Cassell, 1992

Guderian, H., *Panzer Leader*, Penguin Classic edition, 2000

Gunsburg, J. A., 'The Battle of the Belgian Plain, 12–14 May 1940', *Journal of Military History 56*, April 1992

Gunsburg, J. A., 'The Battle of Gembloux, 14–15 May 1940', *Journal of Military History 64*, January 2000

Hamilton, N., *Monty: The Making of a General 1887–1942*, Hamish Hamilton, 1981

Hayward, J., *Myths and Legends of the Second World War*, Sutton, 2003

Hinsley, F. H., *British Intelligence in the Second World War*, Volume I, HMSO, 1979

Horne, A., *To Lose a Battle: France 1940*, Macmillan, 1969

Jackson, J., *The Fall of France: The Nazi Invasion of 1940*, OUP, 2003

Jackson, R., *Dunkirk: The British Evacuation, 1940*, Arthur Barker, 1976

Keegan, J. (editor), *Churchill's Generals*, W & N, 1991

Kershaw, I., *Hitler 1889–1936 Hubris*, Allen Lane, 1998

Kershaw, I., *Hitler 1936–1945 Nemesis*, Allen Lane, 2000

Kesselring, A., *Memoirs of Field Marshal Kesselring*, English edition, William Kimber, 1953

Lacouture, J., *De Gaulle: The Rebel 1890–1944*, English edition, Collins Harvill, 1990

Lewin, R., *Rommel as Military Commander*, Batsford, 1968

Bibliography

Liddell Hart, B. H., *Other side of the Hill*, Cassell, 1948/51

Lukacs, J., *Last European War*, Anchor Press, 1976

Maier, K., Rohde, H., Stegeman, B., and Umbreit, H., *Germany and the Second World War*, Volume II, Oxford, 1991

Masefield, J., *Twenty-Five Days*, 1941

May, E. R., *Strange Victory: Hitler's Conquest of France*, Hill and Wang, 2000

Murray, W. and Millett, A. R. (editors), *Military Innovation in the Inter-war period*, CUP, 1996

Murray, W. and Millett, A. R., *A War to Be Won: Fighting the Second World War*, Harvard UP, 2000

Murray, W., *Luftwaffe: Strategy for Defeat*, Quantum Publishing, 2000

Parker, R. A. C., *Struggle for Survival: The History of The Second World War*, OUP, 1990

Perrett, B., *Lightning War: A History of Blitzkrieg*, Robert Hale, 1983

Sebag-Montefiore, H., *Dunkirk: Fight to the Last Man*, Viking, 2006

Shirer, W., *Collapse of the Third Republic*, Heineman, Secker and Warburg, 1970

Smith, P. C., *Naval Warfare in the English Channel 1939–1945*, Pen and Sword, 2007

Spick, M., *Illustrated Directory of Fighters*, Salamander Books, 2002

Terraine, J., *Right of the Line*, Hodder and Stoughton, 1985

Tombs, R. and I., *That Sweet Enemy: Britain and France*, Heinemann, 2006

Tooze, A., *Wages of Destruction*, Allen Lane, 2006

Trevor-Roper, H. R. (editor), *Hitler's War Directives*, Sidgwick & Jackson, 1964

Warner, P., *Battle of France, 1940*, Simon and Schuster, 1990

Watt, D. C., *Too Serious a Business: European Armed Forces and the Approach to the Second World War*, Norton, 1975

Watt, D. C., *How War Came*, Heinemann, 1989

Weinberg, G. L., *A World at Arms: A Global History of World War II*, CUP, 1994

Wilson, P., *Dunkirk 1940: From Disaster to Deliverance*, Leo Cooper, 1999

Young, R. J., *In Command of France: French Foreign and Military Planning 1933–1940*, Harvard UP, 1978

Index

Index

Index

Index